The Business of Books

V

The Business of Books

How International Conglomerates
Took Over Publishing
and Changed the Way We Read

ANDRÉ SCHIFFRIN

VERSO

London • New York

First published by Verso 2000
Paperback edition published by Verso 2001
© André Schiffrin 2000, 2001

1 3 5 7 9 10 8 6 4 2

VERSO
UK: 6 Meard Street, London W1F 0EG
USA: 180 Varick Street, New York, NY 10014-4606

Verso is the imprint of New Left Books

Design by POLLEN

ISBN 1 85984 362 X

British Library Cataloguing in Publication Data
A catalogue record for this book is available from the British Library

Library of Congress Cataloging-in-Publication Data
A catalog record for this book is available from the Library of Congress

Printed in the UK by Cromwell Press

Contents

Acknowledgments

WARMEST THANKS to Colin Robinson, who first suggested I write this book and then fought mightily and very skillfully to improve it. Warmest thanks also to Sara Bershtel, my former Pantheon colleague, who took time away from her own heavy load of work to help with mine. Thanks, too, to Jessica Blatt and Sarah Fan, who helped piece together my chaotic manuscript. Thanks also to my wife, Maria Elena de la Iglesia, and my daughters, Anya and Natalia — critical but essential first readers.

Thanks are also due to Eric Hazan of La Fabrique, who asked me to write a version of this book that appeared in France last year as *l'Edition sans éditeurs*. Karen Winkler of the *Chronicle of Higher Education* requested that I write a series of articles on publishing, some of which have been transformed into chapters of this book. Katrina vanden Heuvel and Victor Navasky at the *Nation* were the first to ask me to write about the transformation of publishing. Roger Rosenblatt asked me to write a piece for his anthology, *Consuming Desires: Consumption, Culture, and the Pursuit of Happiness*, which included some of my thoughts on paperback publishing.

Although I have edited many, the experience of writing a book has been an education in itself, and I am grateful to all those who worked as teachers with a reluctant and difficult pupil.

Preface to the Paperback Edition

THIS BOOK is an attempt to examine the changing face of the media, particularly book publishing, throughout the world. In recent years, as I will show, the large international conglomerates have taken over an ever-increasing share of publishing in every country. At the same time, a new generation of small, independent publishers has come into being.

Still, in the year since this book originally appeared, the trends I have tried to analyze have continued unabated. In country after country, the few remaining independent publishers have decreased still further in number. In Great Britain, where there were only four important independents, one of the most promising, Fourth Estate, was bought up by HarperCollins, part of the Murdoch empire. Consistent with events described in the chapters on censorship that follow, one of the first decisions taken after the merger was to cancel the contract for a biography of Murdoch, which the publishers realized would be critical of its subject. The impact of Fourth Estate's sale negatively affected other independent publishers. A number of the smaller British firms, such as Granta, Profile, and Verso (the publishers of this book), relied on Fourth Estate's excellent sales force to represent their books to the bookstores. Once the merger had taken place, this was no longer possible and these smaller firms had to find new ways of selling their books. This task became even more difficult with the announcement that the UK's largest bookstore chain, Waterstone's, would demand much higher discounts from smaller firms, a decision that threatened economic ruin for many of them. Appeals to the appropriate authorities in Britain were rejected and at the time of writing this preface it is unclear what will happen next. Interestingly, a similar development has occurred in the U.S. record business, where the giant Tower chain has decided to cut back drastically on its stock of the smaller, classical music labels.

In France, the long-established 19th-century firm of Flammarion, the doyenne of French independent publishers, was bought up by Rizzoli, the Italian publishing arm of the Fiat Corporation, just as last year's Frankfurt Book Fair opened its doors. I have yet to find a French or Italian publisher who can explain the editorial rationale for such a merger. But clearly the urge to diversify internationally, to become a player on the European scene, and in general simply to grow by acquisition is enough to justify mergers that may seem difficult to understand otherwise.

In the United States, the merger between Time Warner and AOL had surprisingly swift consequences. The *New York Times* reported the departure of Little, Brown's publisher shortly after the merger was announced. Little, Brown's list was apparently not sufficiently commercial for the new owners. More ominously, the new merged entity announced that they would transform the nature of CNN, one of the country's few twenty-four-hour international news outlets. Four hundred people were fired immediately amid reports that CNN would place less emphasis on news, more on entertainment — and presumably more on profit. Having safely navigated the shoals of anti-trust scrutiny, the new AOL–Time Warner was clearly intent on being even more profitable than its components.

The list of independent U.S. publishers was reduced when Vivendi, the French water and book company which already controlled a third of French publishers, bought Houghton Mifflin, one of the last major U.S. independents. Few could understand why close to two billion dollars were spent to acquire a company whose educational publishing barely fitted with Vivendi's general program. A group headed by Reed Elsevier likewise bought up Harcourt General. This time Reed's educational and reference focus caused concern for the safety of Harcourt's small but prestigious general list.

It's safe to assume that by the time this edition reaches the bookstores, more such mergers will have taken place. The only question is whether the economic downturn which marked the beginning of 2001 will slow down the trend toward ever larger conglomerates or whether, on the contrary, the increasing economic pressures will force even further amalgamations and greater cutbacks.

The issue of what can be done about all of this differs from country to country. One of the most interesting aspects of the publishing of this book has been watching the various debates that have taken place in the various countries in which it appeared. Some seventeen editions will eventually be published, from Japan to Spain, from Uruguay to Russia. In each country publishers and booksellers have debated the issues it raises and sought differing and new solutions. In Italy, for instance, a series of debates in bookstores across the country led to the introduction of a bill in the Italian senate seeking to protect the independents. These were defined as bookstores where the majority of sales come from the backlist. In other countries, the debate on possible discounting and the future of the fixed price of books continues in a lively fashion.

In some countries such as Spain, critics have disagreed with my suggestions of increased government aid. When this has happened, these critics argue, the result has been nepotism and corruption, as in their film industry. But each country has to find appropriate solutions. Certainly just about everyone could do with better funding for school and public libraries, which alone would suffice to give back to publishing some of the economic underpinning from which it has benefited for many decades.

In most countries there has been widespread discussion as to whether the problems are as severe as I suggest. On the whole, book reviewers, critics, and independent publishers have agreed with the analysis I put forward. In several countries, those still working for the large conglomerates concurred in general but argue that it has not affected the firms for which they are still working. Certainly the nature of the changes that I discuss varies from country to country. In France and Germany the large houses are still publishing a far wider selection of intellectual titles than in neighboring countries, but even there available choices have narrowed. In the U.S. and the UK there is little doubt in my mind, having looked carefully at the catalogs over the past decades, that the changes are very considerable and perhaps permanent.

The area in which critics have differed most markedly with my conclusions is the field of new technology. There are many who feel that electronic publishing will solve many of the problems I describe, but it is evident that the underlying problem of how to get people to pay for materials that appear on the Web has yet to be solved. Even Stephen

King's latest experiments at getting readers to pay for his books in the Dickensian manner of purchasing each chapter separately has not succeeded. King abandoned this attempt when the number of purchases diminished markedly, even though the quantity of would-be purchasers was far greater than most authors would dream of. Perhaps more telling is the fact that the widely read American literary and political magazines that appear on the Web, such as Slate and Salon, have failed to find a way to get people to pay for their service. On March 9, 2001, the *New York Times* ran a detailed analysis showing that the original expectations of substantial income have been very disappointing. Gone were the business plans showing 100,000 subscribers — and profit — in three years. Even though Slate and Salon register millions of hits each month, their editors have failed to find a way of getting people to pay for the use of the magazines; now they are considering the possibility of issuing print versions. Only time will tell whether this solution will work, but it is clearly not a way of dealing with the problems facing books on the Web.

The more optimistic partisans of the Web tend to forget that the most expensive book is not the ten thousandth or even the hundredth copy but the very first. Authors may need years of financial support and editorial help before their work is finished. I well remember my last year at Pantheon when two of the *New York Times Book Review*'s list of the ten best books of the year came from our catalog. Ian Gibson's biography of Lorca and Cameron Watts's marvelous history of the origins of World War II, *How War Came*, had both been commissioned twenty years before we published the books. Clearly the authors needed substantial financial support over those decades, support which we were only able to provide in anticipation of sales. Even the university presses have not yet figured out how the editorial work required in the preparation of monographs to be published online will be covered once the initial foundation grants run out. It is hard enough to make books pay for themselves when they are sold, copy by copy, in bookstores and by mail. The idea that authors can sit down at their computers and simply feed in their major works without outside support is not realistic.

We are still in the early days of the new technologies and it is certainly possible that new ways of dealing with these problems will be discovered. The question remains whether sufficient time, effort, and money will be spent on books that are not significantly profitable in printed form and even less profitable online. These are the books that are often the most important and are the ones most endangered. That, of course, is the story which I try to tell in *The Business of Books*, and I will leave it to the readers to see whether they find themselves convinced by the analysis that follows.

〜

I MENTIONED the fact that *The Business of Books* will appear in a number of countries. This is due to the very considerable efforts of our overseas agents, who have put in far more work than the modest advances have paid for, and I'm very grateful to them. I particularly want to mention Ursula Bender, who has been representing The New Press in Germany since The Press's origins. Ursula was responsible for finding a German publisher for this book and for far more besides. During the many years when she worked at Pantheon as my associate publisher, she was a key figure in the firm's success. Her abilities in the fields of marketing and rights accounted for the success of many of our books. When emphasizing the editorial aspects of what Pantheon accomplished in these pages, I neglected to give her the enormous credit she deserves. I owe her my thanks and apologies for this belated acknowledgment.

Introduction

WHEN RANDOM HOUSE bought the venerable publisher Alfred A. Knopf in 1960, the story was reported on the front page of the *New York Times*. Its appearance caused the attorney general's office to call Bennett Cerf, the head of Random House. On learning that the total value of the merged houses was under $15 million and that their combined share of the market did not reach even 1 percent of total sales, the official expressed surprise that the story should have been given such prominence. Just the other week a similar story made the front page of the *Times* and other papers around the world. America Online's purchase of Time Warner was given full headline treatment, and no one doubted that the $165 billion deal was a major turning point in the history of corporate control of communications. On this occasion, however, the attorney general's office was not on the phone, and every indication suggested that the deal would go through, unhindered by antitrust litigation.

One had to search far into the story to see the small part book publishing played in the AOL purchase, $1.1 billion to be exact. Book publishing, with total annual sales of $23 billion in the United States, is becoming increasingly engulfed in a corporate media structure, where individual companies are worth more than the entire book market. (The AOL purchase price was more than seven times the value of all books sold in America last year. Publishing is rapidly becoming a minor part of the overall communications industry.)

Hardly a week goes by without a new takeover or amalgamation. In the last few months, HarperCollins, owned by Rupert Murdoch, purchased the remnants of the Hearst publishing effort — a move that brought William Morrow and Avon Books into the American holdings of News Corporation. Two months after the takeover, HarperCollins dismissed eighty of Morrow's two hundred employees. The announcement of plans for shared warehousing and other facilities led many to predict Simon & Schuster's absorption into HarperCollins as well. On the other side of town, the German firm of Bertelsmann began the process of consolidating its vast holdings, firing a large number of major executives and assimilating overlapping parts of its empire. Bertelsmann also began negotiations to merge its book clubs under the general direction of The Literary Guild, with the Book-of-the-Month Club now owned by Time Warner. Today, five major conglomerates control 80 percent of American book sales. In 1999, the top twenty publishers accounted for 93 percent of sales, and the ten largest had 75 percent of revenues.[1]

Time Warner, which owns Little, Brown and Company as well as the Book-of-the-Month Club, is the largest of the media conglomerates, with close to $31 billion in sales. It is followed by Disney, whose publishing house is Hyperion, with $24 billion, and now Viacom/CBS, which still owns Simon & Schuster, with nearly $19 billion. Bertelsmann earns $16 billion, 34 percent of which comes from the United States, and all of which derives from publishing and music.[2] Murdoch's News Corporation is the smallest of the big five, with $14 billion, of which HarperCollins accounts for a mere $764 million.[3]

These media empires have grown very rapidly. In 1988, Disney took in less than $3 billion a year, primarily from its films and amusement parks; Time only $4 billion; and Warner just $3 billion. Viacom did a paltry $600 million worth of business just twelve years ago.[4] The growth of these giants is due largely to takeovers that have left very few publishing houses independent, as we shall see.

Now that virtually all of American life is affected by the seemingly never-ending growth of large corporations, it is fair to ask how much all of this matters. Is what we are witnessing truly something new or merely a variation on an old theme? Will it change fundamentally the way we read and what books are available to us? After all, some seventy thousand books were published in the United States last year. Is that not enough for every conceivable taste?

Large publishers have always been with us. And looking back to the nineteenth century, we see substantial book sales then, too — numbers that, in proportion to population, are often greater than today's. But the story of publishing is much more than a list of sales figures. The important questions are what was being published, what choices were available, and what new ideas, whether in fiction or nonfiction, were being offered to the public. The story also raises issues about the relationship of high culture to mass audiences during a still-evolving industrialization. How were the book houses themselves transformed and what was the effect of the changes on people working in publishing?

It would have been helpful in writing this book if extensive research were available to document the specifics of these changes. Unfortunately, very few general histories of American publishing exist and these are generally broad surveys. There are a few memoirs — surprisingly few — a handful of biographies of famous American and British publishers, and a few corporate histories. Some, like Eugene Exman's book on Harper's, are admirably frank and fascinating; others are more in the nature of public relations exercises.[5] For the most part, this book is based on my own experiences in publishing. I have also spoken with a large number of my colleagues, both in the United States and abroad, about how their careers have been altered by the changes in the industry.

I want to describe a small but, I hope, indicative part of this story, focusing on how American publishing has changed over the last half century. I will begin in the early 1940s, when my father, Jacques Schiffrin, helped to found a small exile publishing house in New York called Pantheon Books, which, in the twenty years of its independent existence, brought much European writing to the United States. For reasons I'll describe later, I found myself unexpectedly following in his footsteps. In the thirty years I worked at

Pantheon I saw both the achievements and failures of independent publishing and its ultimate disappearance as a major force. The developments of recent years have shown that the Pantheon story was not as unique as many initially thought. It is of interest as an early example of a pattern that has now become commonplace.

Before starting at Pantheon, I worked for one of the large American mass-market paperback houses, the New American Library, which was owned and inspired by the British company Penguin Books. This experience informs my understanding of the transformation of mass-market publishing, particularly in the United States and Britain, something I consider to be an important chapter in the history of mass culture. A decade ago, after leaving Pantheon, I started a small, independent, public-interest publishing house, The New Press, whose first years suggest a possible alternative to the increased conglomerate control of publishing.

IN EUROPE and in America, publishing has a long tradition as an intellectually and politically engaged profession. Publishers have always prided themselves on their ability to balance the imperative of making money with that of issuing worthwhile books. In recent years, as the ownership of publishing has changed, that equation has been altered. It is now increasingly the case that the owner's *only* interest is in making money and as much of it as possible. It is widely assumed today that approaches employed lucratively in the entertainment industry will yield similar results when applied to publishing. The standards of the entertainment industry are also apparent in the content of best-seller lists, an ever-narrower range of books based on lifestyle and celebrity with little intellectual or artistic merit.

In the first half of the twentieth century, the assumption that most people only want diversion did not always hold sway (though both George Orwell's *1984* and Aldous Huxley's *Brave New World*, written in the 1930s and 1940s, were most perceptive in envisaging such a society). This was a time when many publishers clearly saw it as their mission to reach a large audience through serious work. During World War II, publishing shared in the mobilization of the population, aiming to support the war effort as well as entertain soldiers and wearied production workers. This sense of optimistic civil engagement persisted until the beginning of the Cold War, when publishing largely followed the lead of other media in drawing the battle lines in an increasingly polarized world.

The end of the Cold War has not had a beneficial intellectual influence on publishing or, indeed, on any of the other media. We have lost much of our curiosity about the communist world and the Third World, curiosity that once provided raw material for a great many important books. But we have seen the development of a new ideology, one that has replaced that of the Western democracies against the Soviet bloc. Belief in the market, faith in its ability to conquer everything, a willingness to surrender all other values to it — and even the belief that it represents a sort of consumer democracy—these things have become the hallmark of publishing.

It is safe to say that publishing has changed more in the last ten years than in the entirety of the previous century. These changes are most obvious in English-speaking countries, which are in many ways models of what is likely to happen in the rest of the world in the coming years. Until quite recently, publishing houses were for the most part family owned and small, content with the modest profits that came from a business that still saw itself as linked to intellectual and cultural life. In recent years, publishers have been put on a procrustean bed and made to fit one of two patterns: as purveyors of entertainment or of hard information. This has left little room for books with new, controversial ideas or challenging literary voices.

More about this process will be found later in this book, but for now it is worth noting just how large the business has become. The media industries are vital to the American economy; they are second only to the aircraft industry in generating the nation's exports. Given the major role that the military has had in developing and maintaining American aviation, it may be said that media products are the largest civilian export. Some 50,000 entities are still recognized by the Library of Congress as publishers. About 5 percent of those, or 2,600, are substantial enough to be recognized by the Association of American Publishers, the trade association. In 1998 close to 2.5 billion books were sold in the United States — far more than in any other Western country — earning some $23 billion. But sheer size does not guarantee diversity of content. On the contrary — more and more of the books published duplicate each other. And although the United States' title output (70,000 new books a year) looks impressive at first glance, it is actually lower per capita than many other countries'. An equal number of books is published in England, which has one-fifth of America's population. France, with a population roughly a quarter of the U.S.'s, issues 20,000 titles, while Finland produces 13,000, of which 1,800 are fiction.

If we look back into America's past, it's surprising to see how much healthier book publishing used to be. In the 1940s, for example, an average issue of the *New York Times Book Review* was sixty-four pages long, twice the length of the current Sunday section. Hundreds of publishing houses had books reviewed and advertised in those pages. The infrastructure of small publishing houses and independent bookstores and book clubs that existed in the 1940s was capable of reaching a very large audience effectively. The changes of recent decades have not been motivated by the need for higher efficiency or greater effectiveness. They have come about through a change of ownership and purpose.

In the 1850s, *Harper's* boasted that "literature has gone in pursuit of the millions, penetrated highways and hedges, pressed its way into cottages, factories, omnibuses and railway cars and become the most cosmopolitan thing of the century."[6] Popular novels like those of now-forgotten Mary Jane Holmes sold some 2 million copies, and were reprinted in batches of 50,000 — this when the country's population was one-twentieth of what it is now. James Hart's very useful history, *The Popular Book: A History of America's Literary Trade*, is filled with figures that are astonishing by today's standards. Books not only had enormous sales but exercised powerful influence. One of the most famous opinion-changers, *Uncle Tom's Cabin*, sold 100,000 copies in its first months and 300,000 in its first year (the equivalent of 6 million copies today), galvanizing public opinion against slavery. Miners in the gold fields of California would pay twenty-five cents, a considerable sum in those days, to borrow the book overnight. The works of Henry George, the economic theorist who argued for a "single tax" on the increased value of property, sold tremendously well: 2 million of his famous *Progress and Poverty*, 3 million of the others. These books not only attracted a vast readership, but, like Edward Bellamy's famous utopian novel, *Looking Backward* (which sold over a million copies around 1900 in the United States and England), inspired social movements. Discussion groups and clubs were created throughout the country to put the ideas in these pages into action.

Many of the most popular books at the turn of the nineteenth century are now considered literary classics. The books most widely borrowed from public libraries were by Sir Walter Scott, Charles Dickens, Leo Tolstoy, William Makepeace Thackeray, Nathaniel Hawthorne, James Fenimore Cooper, Edward George Earle Lytton, and George Eliot. During the 1920s, often thought of as a period of Babbitt-like uniformity, a widespread debate raged in intellectual circles on the dangers of conformity and indeed on the very idea of best-sellers. Sinclair Lewis refused the Pulitzer Prize for *Arrowsmith*, objecting to the concept of a best book or author, a critique that was echoed widely in the press. The Book-of-the-Month Club, in its early days, found its editorial choices subject to criticism from intellectuals, a debate followed in detail in Janice Radway's *A Feeling for Books*.[7]

Through the 1920s and 1930s, some of the most widely read books were highly critical of the ethos of their time. Sinclair Lewis's *Main Street* sold 400,000 copies in 1920; Lytton Strachey's *Queen Victoria* sold 200,000. Similar demand for serious work existed in Europe. *Buddenbrooks* by Thomas Mann sold over a million copies in Germany alone, where Erich Maria Remarque's *All Quiet on the Western Front* achieved equivalent sales.[8]

With the coming of World War II, readers turned to more political books. In 1940, Adolf Hitler's *Mein Kampf* was a best-seller, as were the "Inside" books by John Gunther and Ernest Hemingway's *For Whom the Bell Tolls*, set during the Spanish Civil War, which had sold a million copies by 1946. William Shirer's *Berlin Diary* sold 500,000 copies in 1941 and Wendell Wilkie's programmatic *One World* sold a million. Americans started reading books by Walter Lippmann and Sumner Welles, by former ambassadors such as Joseph Grew (Japan) and Joseph Davies (Russia), whose *Mission to Moscow* became a notorious Hollywood film. In addition to the millions of books bought by civilians, 119 million paperbacks were distributed free in special editions for the armed forces.

It's only in the period immediately after the war that we begin to see America's reading hitting the doldrums. A study published in 1949 under the auspices of the Social Science Research Council[9] showed that reading was falling into a predictable pattern. Of the twenty top fiction best-sellers in 1947, only one author had not been on a previous list. The most popular authors that year were a veritable honor roll of middlebrow culture: Thomas Costain, whose *The Black Rose* had sold 1.3 million in the previous year, Kenneth Roberts, Somerset Maugham, Samuel Shellaburger, A. J. Cronin, John P. Marquand, James Hilton, and Frank Yerby, whose *Little Foxes* sold 1.2 million. (Only John Steinbeck and Sinclair Lewis offered somewhat more demanding fare.) The movie tie-in to *Duel in the Sun* by Nevin Busch sold a phenomenal 2.3 million. The nonfiction best-seller lists were dominated by equally middlebrow and popular titles, including Will Durant's *Story of Philosophy*, Hendrik Van Loon's *The Story of Mankind*, and the omnipresent Dale Carnegie's book about making friends and influencing people, which sold over a million copies in hardcover and over 2 million in a Pocket Books paperback edition.

At this time, most publishing houses still belonged to the people who started them; only a few had grown into publicly held companies. To be sure, the majority of publishers in the United States and Europe were interested in profit as well as literature. But it was understood that entire categories of books, particularly new fiction and poetry, were bound to lose money. It was assumed that believing in authors was an investment for the future and that they would remain faithful to the publishers who had discovered and nourished them. Poaching authors from other firms was not considered fair play. Overall, trade publishers reckoned they would lose money or at best break even on their trade books. Profit would come from subsidiary rights — sales to book clubs or paperback publishers.

Even some of the mass-market publishing houses were trying to broaden the boundaries, to seek new readers, and to raise general levels of literacy and knowledge. The most notable of these was the New American Library of World Literature, where I began my own work in publishing. NAL was initially the American branch of the British Penguin, to whom its general approach to publishing owed a great deal. Penguin was the most successful and influential of the early mass-market publishers, and its policies were emulated throughout Europe and the Americas. Started in the 1930s by a practical businessman called Allen Lane, it hired a number of talented and dedicated chief editors, among whom was V. K. Krishna Menon, later to become India's controversial and committed ambassador to the United Nations. As has been widely discussed, notably in Richard Hoggart's

The Uses of Literacy, Penguin set out to provide the British reading public not only with the best in contemporary fiction but with a range of substantial, educative titles as well. In its Pelican series, Penguin commissioned an impressive range of original work on science, the social sciences, and even the history of art. For the most part, these books had a markedly progressive slant and were often closely linked to the politics of the British left at the time, although they were aimed at a mainstream audience and did not have any particular party bias. Penguin set out to create histories of each of the major countries, books on contemporary public affairs, and a whole range of titles that provided information and ideas for the majority of English people, who had no access to education beyond the age of sixteen. (In 1957, when I was a graduate student at Cambridge University, 83 percent of English youngsters left school at that age.) Penguin's success was a major force in English society in the 1930s and 1940s and helped to create the support that lead to an overwhelming Labour victory at the end of the war.

Those on the left were not the only ones concerned with the problems of reaching a mass readership. The battle for that audience was a hard-fought one, a story yet to be explored in the literature of publishing. The British chain of bookstores and newsstands, W. H. Smith, which began in the 1850s, maintained control over the kinds of books for sale to the general public with a stern conservative eye. Even as late as the 1960s, Smith's attracted notoriety for banning mildly subversive journals such as *Private Eye* and keeping a close watch on what might reach susceptible readers.

The great French publishing and distribution monopoly of Hachette followed the early British example carefully and set up a similar chain of bookstores, also based on newsstands, in the country's major railway stations. But since France in the 1850s was still very much a dictatorship, Hachette had to promise that it would not distribute anything that the government might dislike and specifically that it "would ban all publications which might excite political passions as well as any writings contrary to morality." These included Ernest Renan's *Life of Jesus*, the writings of socialists, other works that might encourage the subversion of public order, and any books suspected of libertine tendencies.[10]

One of the ways around this conservative control of book chains was finding alternative channels of distribution. This was done successfully in Britain by the Left Book Club, created by the popular publisher Victor Gollancz. Gollancz's titles were often aligned politically with the Communist Party. George Orwell's early books, such as *The Road to Wigan Pier*, were published by the Left Book Club while some of his other works, including *Homage to Catalonia*, were rejected by its editorial board because of their justifiably harsh criticism of Russia. (These were published by more independent leftist publishers, in this case Secker & Warburg.) But in spite of its party-line adherence, the Left Book Club enlisted some fifty thousand members and supplied hundreds of thousands of scholarly and important studies to a vast population. The works of Edgar Snow, such as *Red Star Over China*, came out under this imprint, as did major books explaining the rise of German fascism and the coming conflict in Europe. Such books would sell in the tens of thousands at prices very close to Penguin's and helped to create a well-informed vanguard of public opinion on the left. Today such titles are issued in tiny university press editions at prohibitively high prices because of the assumption that a mass audience simply does not exist for them. But the experience of the 1930s, clearly helped by the general political impetus of society at the time, showed that a very large audience could be engaged with demanding books on political issues that often must have seemed very far from the daily cares of most readers. Gollancz, a highly energetic and effective propagandist, reached beyond his primary market. One paperback by John Strachey, *Why You Should Be a Socialist*, sold 300,000 copies at two pence each. In 1938, seeing the possible onset of war, Gollancz went further still in search of an audience, publishing anti-Nazi leaflets for free distribution, one in a printing of 2 million, and another of 10 million.

But Gollancz and the broad range of intellectuals trying to stop Hitler would not succeed. The blitzkrieg soon saw German troops occupying most of Europe, bringing extensive and horrific changes and driving a number of refugees from Europe to the United States.

ONE

Good Reading for the Few
and for the Millions

NEW YORK in 1941 had a tiny French colony. It consisted largely of people who had come to America before the war and were mostly involved in the restaurant trade and other small businesses. To this number now was added a group of exiled intellectual and political figures, for the most part far more determined in their opposition to the Vichy regime than were those who had emigrated before. Accordingly, the French community was divided into those who were in favor of Philippe Pétain; those who, like many of their compatriots in France, were waiting to see what would happen and who could best be described as *attentistes*; and the small number committed either to Charles de Gaulle or to his rival, General Henri Giraud.[11]

The Rockefeller Foundation and other institutions attempted to obtain visas for French scholars and place them in American universities. For the most part, however, these efforts were doubly frustrated, first by a state department that was determined at all costs to keep down the number of Jewish refugees from Europe, and also by strong opposition on the part of many American universities. Major institutions such as Harvard, which might have been expected to welcome refugee scholars, put up massive, openly xenophobic, and anti-Semitic resistance. Though, in this way, the exiles' number and influence was limited, an important intellectual presence would soon be established by Claude Lévi-Strauss, Georges Gourevitch, and others; a university-in-exile would be created at New York's New School.

In spite of quotas and other obstacles, hundreds of thousands of refugees came to America before the beginning of the European War. The largest group — some 300,000 — came from Germany and Austria. Among these were a number of distinguished publishers, several of whom sought to establish their own publishing houses in exile. A few, such as the Fischer Verlag family, continued to publish in German. Others sought to create lists in English, sometimes in fields very different from those that had occupied them in their homeland. L. Kagan, for instance, the publisher of the Berlin firm Petropolis, who had been known in Europe in the 1920s for publishing the Russian literary exiles of the period, found himself reincarnated as the head of the newly founded International University's press, which specialized in Freudian psychoanalytical literature. Most importantly for my story, Kurt Wolff, who had been one of the most distinguished German publishers in the 1920s and 1930s, renowned for his original publication of Franz Kafka, started Pantheon Books in New York in 1942 with his wife, Helen, and an American partner, Kyrill Schabert. My father, Jacques, would soon join them.

Born in Russia in 1892, my father went to France shortly after World War I, where he began a career as a publisher and translator. With very limited resources, he began publishing French classics and, with his new friend André Gide, he translated a number of Russian classics into French, editions of which are still in print. He called his publishing house Editions de La Pléiade and in the 1930s went on to conceive the now famous Pléiade collection of the world's classics. The original aim of the Pléiade was to make the best literature available at accessible prices, though today the series is sold in luxurious editions.

The venture was so successful that my father's limited capital soon became inadequate. He turned to Editions Gallimard, joining them in 1936 to direct the Pléiade within their much more substantial framework. I believe he expected to spend the rest of his working life with Gallimard. But the war intervened, and though he was in his late forties, my father was drafted into the French army. Shortly after the occupation of France, he discovered that the new German "ambassador," Otto Abetz, had a list of people, primarily Jews, who were to be purged from the French cultural scene. Abetz had worked in France before the war and was very familiar with its intellectual and social life. He once stated that the key institutions in France were the bank, the communist party, and Gallimard.[12] To be useful to Abetz, Gallimard had to be aryanized. My father was the only well-known Jew working for the firm, and shortly after the French defeat on August 20, 1940, he received a two-line letter from Gallimard informing him that he was no longer in their employ. Though this act was committed under direct pressure from the German occupying forces, the Gallimard family understandably preferred to forget it, and for many years no mention was made of my father's role in bringing the Pléiade to Gallimard or of his subsequent departure. The Pléiade has since become the backbone of Gallimard's publishing. Even after the publication of the French version of the present book last year,[13] Gallimard continues to deny what had happened during the war, claiming to the press that my father had left France in 1939, in spite of all the evidence to the contrary. An important account of these events can be found in an excellent history of French publishing under German occupation by Pascal Fouché.[14]

As a Jew of foreign origin and one who had already been singled out as such, my father understandably felt that staying in France would mean living under a death sentence. After being demobilized from the French army, he spent the following year in an agonizing search for visas, departure permits, and tickets to safety for himself, his wife, Simone, and his six-year-old son — myself. This led us on the well-traveled route from northern occupied France into the unoccupied southern zone, where for some months we lived in an apartment in St. Tropez that had been our vacation home. Finally, thanks to the intervention of the heroic American "pimpernel" Varian Fry, who had been sent to France to help a number of intellectuals clearly at risk, the requisite papers were drawn up and we left from Marseilles on a boat to Casablanca in the spring of 1941. Most of our fellow passengers were German exiles. I still remember the trays of swastika-bearing passports on the ship's deck. When we arrived, the Vichy French government hypocritically insisted that Casablanca's hotels would be overburdened by refugees and that we would have to be relocated to the desert, where living conditions were terrible. Thanks to the intervention of Gide, who lent us his apartment in Casablanca, we were spared these desert concentration camps. After some months of waiting in Casablanca, we progressed to Lisbon, arriving in New York in August 1941. It was there that, within a few months, my father took up the challenge of publishing again, in French, in a foreign country.

In 1942, with a small amount of capital from friends, he began a series of books under his own name, which brought the writings of the French Resistance to America for the first time. *Les Silences de la mer* by Vercors was published in New York shortly after the RAF had distributed copies over France. Other books of resistance writing included Joseph Kessel's *L'Armée des ombres* and a collection of Louis Aragon's poetry, published in paperback covers in the French manner. These books gave the French in the New World some link to what was happening in Europe, and contracts for several titles were soon drawn up with similarly minded publishers in Latin America. Victoria Ocampo of Ediciones del Sur in Buenos Aires was among those who closely followed what was being published by the New York exiles, and in time Argentine editions of a number of these books were issued.

As a boy I often went down to visit my father in his offices. While, like many children, I was fascinated by my father's work, it didn't occur to me that I might follow in his footsteps. His various skills, including facility with many languages and the ability to design beautiful books, seemed completely beyond my own. Although I enjoyed listening to the conversations at home with his fellow exiles such as Hannah Arendt and the few Americans my parents had befriended, their concerns seemed far from my adolescent world. I was certainly not one of those publishing offspring who assume that their parent's firm is automatically a part of their future. The experience of exile was dramatic and suggested a world lost, never to be retrieved.

Later in the same year, shortly after the founding of Pantheon Books, my father joined forces with Kurt Wolff. Pantheon had already begun to publish a list of austere literary and cultural importance in both English and German. The company offices were an unlikely oasis on Washington Square in New York, in one of the Georgian houses that used to border the park on the south, known as "genius row" for this small group of Europeans who struggled to discover what aspects of their culture might be accepted by American readers. It occurs to me as I write that I never knew what language they spoke together— was it French or German? Certainly it would not have been English.

Pantheon's early commercial successes were few, though it soon began to publish important literary work. Gide sent his *Intervues imaginaires* from Tunisia as well as *Theseus*, both published for the first time in my father's French-language series, as was Camus's *L'Etranger*, which Knopf would later publish in English. The Wolffs likewise sought to publish exemplars of German culture such as the poems of Stefan George, which they issued in a bilingual edition, a book one can well imagine was read by only a tiny number of Americans. Other translations included works by Paul Claudel, Charles Péguy, Georges Bernanos and Jacques Maritain. But while the French- and German-reading audiences were enthusiastic purchasers of the books published for them, their numbers were limited and the American public remained largely ignorant of such work.

That refugees were far more interested in Pantheon's output than the native population was demonstrated by the demand for Hermann Broch's *The Death of Virgil*. Broch had been one of the leading experimental novelists of interwar Europe, and his first novel, *The Sleepwalker*, was considered one of the most important books of that time. After the Nazi takeover, he was arrested by the Gestapo and imprisoned for five months. He was finally able to escape with the help of James Joyce and others. In America he wrote his next major novel, *The Death of Virgil*. Pantheon published this admittedly demanding book in two editions — 1,500 copies were printed in English and the same number in German. The German edition sold out immediately; it took over twenty years for the English-language copies to be sold.

In addition to traditional American isolationism, Pantheon had to contend with the anti-German hostility of the war years. A case in point was their publication of the first complete translation of the Grimm fairy tales. While a number of reviewers dealt civilly with the book, others took it as an opportunity to write long comments on the inherent brutality of the German soul. But the integrity of Pantheon's early output was appreciated by a few discerning commentators. Helmut Lehmann-Haupt, the father of the current *New York Times* daily book critic, wrote in *The Book in America*:

> The very significant thing about Pantheon Books is the fact that it has not issued a single trivial or merely popular title, not a book chosen primarily because of its profit-making possibilities. Every book on the list is of unquestionable cultural value or of decided artistic significance, or a genuine attempt to contribute to the solution of the intellectual and spiritual dilemma of these difficult years.[15]

Of course, Lehmann-Haupt was himself a part of the exile generation that followed Pantheon's list.

With the end of the war there was renewed interest in the press about what was going on in Europe. The *New York Times*, for instance, would often devote one of its book review pages to a

literary letter from a European capital. American interest in foreign fiction, however, did not reflect this shift. It was not until the
1950s that Simone de Beauvoir's *The Mandarins* would hit the
best-seller list, the only such success for decades.

In the meantime, and quite unexpectedly, an unlikely group of
esoteric titles brought Pantheon its greatest commercial success.
Influenced by their life in the Weimar Republic, the Wolffs shared the
German interest of that time in Eastern thought and religions.
Accordingly, they were among the first to publish books on Zen
Buddhism in the United States. One of these, *Zen and the Art of
Archery*, by the German scholar Eugen Herrigel, became a perennial
best-seller for Pantheon. A book on how to practice archery with neither bow nor arrow was bound to cause a certain amount of incredulity
—the buyers of New York's most fashionable sporting goods shop,
Abercrombie & Fitch, who agreed to take a few copies, were unsure
as to whether it would undermine the sale of their archery equipment
—but it caught the public's imagination and went on to sell hundreds
of thousands of copies.

Another unexpected early windfall came through Mary Mellon, the
wife of the millionaire philanthropist and art collector Paul Mellon,
whose father, Andrew, was former secretary of the treasury and United
States National Gallery donor. Mary had been psychoanalyzed by C.
G. Jung and wanted to pay homage to him by creating a series that
brought together his collected works in English as well as the books
of noted Jungian scholars, many of them also German exiles.

It is intriguing to imagine the relationship between one of
America's wealthiest women and Pantheon's partners, who were two
impressive but clearly impoverished European intellectuals. A fam-

ily legend tells of Mary's first visit to my father's small office over-looking Washington Square. He was signing a letter and briefly looked up to say, "Please have a seat." After he kept her waiting for a few minutes longer, presumably on purpose, Mary cleared her throat and said, "Perhaps you don't realize who I am. I'm Mary Mellon." Whereupon my father answered, "Oh, I'm terribly sorry; please take two seats." Whether apocryphal or not, the story suggests he wanted to make it clear that Mary's wealth did not mean that she was to be a patron and he merely a client. Both Kurt Wolff and my father were to play an active role in suggesting titles and helping to form this new and unique publishing venture.

With the Mellons' substantial support, Pantheon began to pub-lish the Bollingen series, named after Jung's country home. My father designed the early Bollingen books, including the collected poems of St. Jean Perse, which remain to this day an extraordinary example of what can be achieved when money and taste are com-bined to good effect. Paul Rand was responsible for many of the covers, and the series as a whole earned a reputation as some of the most beautiful books ever published in the United States.

Although the Bollingen series played an unanticipated and important role in mainstream American culture in the years that followed, its original works were erudite and highly demanding. Wolff and my father made a substantial effort to publish the writings of exiled intellectuals whenever they could be fitted into the Bollingen framework. One of the first such books was by Max Raphael, a Marxist art critic my father had known in France.

In time, books that strayed from the Jungian path found their way onto the list. My father arranged for the publication of André Malraux's three-volume *Psychology of Art* and the collected works of Paul Valéry and Miguel Unamuno. Because of Jung's influence and the Wolffs' interests in the East, such works as Heinrich Zimmer's massive study of Indian art were also published. This was followed by Joseph Campbell's works, which became extraordinarily influential in the 1960s. But such unexpected successes were dwarfed when the Bollingen series, reflecting Jungian interest in world religions, issued the first complete translation of the *I Ching*. A more esoteric volume would be hard to imagine, but it had already influenced composers such as John Cage and other intellectuals interested in the relationship of chance and probability to everyday life. The book proved to be a perfect companion to the budding counterculture of the 1960s and sold an enormous number of copies—over a million in hardcover. In this way, the refugee publishers made an unexpected contribution to popular culture, while their dedicated efforts to bring the best of a European literary tradition to American readers went largely unnoticed.

My father's health had been severely impaired during the war when, as a relatively older soldier, he suffered from the harsh conditions of military life. His ill health had prevented him from returning to France at the end of war, as he had originally hoped to do, and it deteriorated further during the late 1940s. In 1950 he died of emphysema, and with his death the family links to Pantheon were severed, I assumed forever. I continued to follow Pantheon's fortunes from a distance and watched as they were dramatically altered by a series of unforeseen events.

One such had taken place in Aspen, Colorado, in 1949, where Kurt Wolff had been invited to a celebration marking the centennial of Goethe's death organized by another German exile, the designer,

Paepke, a major influence on the American Can Corporation, one of America's largest corporations. By happenstance, Wolff was seated next to Anne Morrow Lindbergh, whose links to Germany are best forgotten (her husband, Charles, became notorious in the 1930s as one of the leading American advocates of an isolationist, pro-German, and even anti-Semitic position). Wolff discovered that Anne was at work on a collection of contemplative essays. Published as *Gift from the Sea*, it became a phenomenal best-seller and was one of the successes that would lead to Pantheon's transformation.

Then, in the late 1950s, Pantheon took on a difficult Russian novel and printed 4,000 copies. The award of the Nobel Prize to its author, Boris Pasternak, turned *Dr. Zhivago* into an international best-seller, and Pantheon found itself overwhelmed with orders, selling over a million copies in hardcover and a further 5 million in paperback. Its success was followed by that of Giuseppe di Lampedusa's *The Leopard*, and within a few months Pantheon was transformed from a struggling, marginal firm into an excessively profitable one.

As is so often the case, money was to change the firm's future irrevocably. Disagreements began to arise between the Wolffs and their American partner, and they decided to move back to Europe, settling in Switzerland, from where they hoped to continue to direct the firm's editorial fortunes. Such an arrangement would have been difficult under the best of circumstances but, with the growing tensions between the founders, it proved impossible and the original partnership soon broke up. The Wolffs moved on to an affiliation with Harcourt Brace, where they continued publishing for many years. Deprived of their editorial leadership, Pantheon's shareholders decided that the time had come to sell up, and they found a willing purchaser in Bennett Cerf, the head of Random House. Cerf's company had gone public in 1959 and, flush with cash, had bought the distinguished firm of Alfred A. Knopf, known for its serious books on American life and history as well as its successful list of translations. As a result, Random had become one of the most important publishers in the United States. The purchase of Pantheon in 1961 (for less than $1 million) added an important element to the collective backlist of the Random empire and seemed a promising new beginning for its latest acquisition.

❧

WHILE I KEPT track of Pantheon's progress from afar, I never expected to find a job there. The Wolffs had their own sons, who I assumed would follow in their footsteps. But I was drawn to publishing and was particularly interested in the kind of books that reach a mass audience. In the summers, while still at college, I worked part-time at New American Library and, in 1959, was offered a full-time job there, in the college marketing department.

The books published by NAL were very much the heirs of the general tradition pioneered by Penguin, which sought to provoke intellectual and political debate on a wide scale. The Penguin editors and, later, those at NAL, felt that crucial issues were not meant to be decided simply by an elite group of experts and politicians, assuming that the population as a whole would be interested and deeply involved in the debates. I remember as a schoolchild receiving the newspaper *My Weekly Reader*, which was sent to youngsters of ages twelve and up; it had discussions on what the future of

America's policy should be on issues such as public housing and rural electrification. It was part of the euphoria and optimism of the postwar period that even schoolchildren were presumed to be interested in subjects that would be dismissed today as too esoteric and remote for all but a tiny number of adults.

NAL was a major publisher of paperback books. In the United States, cheap paperback editions had begun to be popular in the late 1930s, pioneered by Pocket Books. The new paperbacks were distributed to the four thousand bookstores that covered the United States at this time and to nonbookstore outlets as well — the famous cigar stores, newsstands, drugstores, and the like — which numbered seventy thousand. These had been part of the old magazine distribution network, started after Prohibition by former bootleggers such as Annenberg, initially to distribute the racing form. These new distributors soon moved on to a broader range of magazines and later into the book business, with much success. They treated books like periodicals, returning unsold copies at the end of the month. This new system worked extremely well and resulted in phenomenal sales. The NAL's most successful title ever, Erskine Caldwell's *Tobacco Road*, sold 4 million copies in its first two years, with the rest of Caldwell's work selling a further 4 million. James T. Farrell's *Studs Lonigan*, which had sold a mere 500 copies as a hardcover in its first year of publication, sold 350,000 in paperback. Close to 50 million paperbacks were bought annually, roughly a fifth of all the books sold. A substantial number of readers of regular trade books quickly became attached to the new paperback format. Such books were often based on the old popular magazines such as *True Detective* and *True Romance*, as well as on short westerns. In the 1940s, 10 million magazines were sold every week, as well as a phenomenal 25 million comics, so proper books, even in their new formats, were still a relatively small percentage of the reading matter being sold to the country as a whole.[16]

To a large degree, the new paperback lists of the 1940s replicated the lowbrow commercialism of best-sellers in the previous decade. Books like Thornton Wilder's *The Bridge at San Luis Rey*, the novels of Zane Grey, and highly popular books like *Forever Amber* repeated their initial hardcover sales in paperback. However, NAL saw its task as going beyond the westerns and the thrillers and began to make available a far more intellectual selection. Following the example of Penguin's Pelican imprint, they launched the Mentor series under the slogan "good reading for the millions."

NAL published all of William Faulkner and a number of contemporary realist European authors, such as Curzio Malaparte and Pier Paolo Pasolini. Among their early books were *Martin Eden*, Jack London's radical classic, and Carson McCullers's *The Heart Is a Lonely Hunter*. At the same time, readers of the Mentor series could buy Margaret Mead's *Coming of Age in Samoa* or Marquis Child's *Sweden: The Middle Way*, as well as a long list of political titles. I remember as a teenager buying a Mentor book called *The Christian Demand for Social Justice*, not a title you'd find in today's airport newsstands.

These paperbacks cost twenty-five to thirty-five cents, the price of a pack of cigarettes. One of the most expensive books we published was James T. Farrell's *Lonigan Trilogy*. It was so long that we had to charge fifty cents for it. The sales people finally decided that the book's spine should be broken into bands, so that the customer could see that he was getting two books' worth and would not feel ripped off.

The jackets of these paperbacks were uniformly lurid. If you did not look at the title, you would be hard pressed to know whether what you had in your hand was by Mickey Spillane or by William Faulkner. Even though Faulkner was described on all of his paperback covers as the author of *Sanctuary*, a book widely read for its highly charged sexual content, the entirety of his work was, in fact, available. It would be many years before his books would become a staple of college courses, ironically losing most of their popular audience as they became elevated to the canon.

NAL was run by a very odd couple indeed, two characters who could not have been more different. Victor Weybright, the chief editor, was a large, flamboyant man who gloried in his snobberies and pretensions. His walls were covered by the usual photographs of authors but also by portraits of himself in the shocking pink of the Maryland Hunt. He was a man of varied enthusiasms (and, as his memoirs were to show, of unmitigated anti-Semitism) but he surrounded himself with some brilliant editors. Kurt Enoch, the president in charge of the commercial end, was small, trim, very shy, and a model German intellectual. In Europe, he had been among the first to understand the potential of the modern paperback and had created the famous Tauschnitz editions in English, which, until a few years ago, could still be found in secondhand bookshops throughout Europe. Enoch had originally hired me through connections of my father's and such was the rivalry between the two partners that, being tarred by this brush, I could never expect to become part of the editorial group. However, Weybright allowed me to sit in on the group's discussions. The editors included Ed Doctorow (before he became famous as a novelist); Mark Jaffe, who was to become a major paperback publisher in his own right; and Arabel Porter, a quiet and unpretentious intellectual who was responsible for the success of the paperback literary review *New World Writing*. Modeled on the famous British paperback series New Writing, which was edited by John Lehmann and published by Penguin during the war, *New World Writing* was animated by the belief that ordinary people could read challenging, daring work and ought to be able to find it in every drugstore. An early issue offered a selection of contemporary Korean poetry. Despite such esoteric subject matter the magazine had initial printings of up to 75,000 copies. Such was its success that other paperback publishers launched their own rival versions and for a few years, the American public was offered an unprecedented selection of avant-garde literary material.

NAL paperbacks could be issued with great speed when the need arose. Doctorow remembers commissioning a book on the Eichmann case, which was rushed to the stores in a few weeks and went on to sell half a million copies. This kind of publishing blurred the line between books and news magazines and was made possible because they were available through the same distribution system.

Paperback publishers continued to play the role of commentators on current affairs well into the 1960s. At the height of the McCarthy period, Bantam Books published Owen Lattimore's self-defense, a courageous act at the time given the viciousness with which McCarthy had attacked Lattimore as one of those who had "lost China." As late as the Vietnam War, Bantam and other mass-market companies published collections of political essays and criticism written for the broader public. Ballantine pioneered original work along political lines, publishing C. Wright Mills's *Listen Yankee* in 1960.

Though my responsibilities were not formally editorial, I was able to persuade NAL to take on a major series. Looking at the books being used in schools, it seemed to me that there could be an enormous audience for inexpensive paperback editions of the world's classics. The Modern Library had done this in hardcover, but these were relatively expensive books compared to the twenty-five or thirty-five cents that we could charge for editions of *Huckleberry Finn* or *Crime and Punishment*. I sent a memo to Arabel Porter suggesting what I thought could be the first books in what later became the Signet Classic series, together with potential authors of scholarly introductions that would make the books more useful in schools and colleges. The idea received a favorable response and was developed in ways that made it more realistic, with American classics such as *Tom Sawyer* being added to my somewhat esoteric initial selection. One of my original proposals was the nineteenth-century French classic, Benjamin Constant's *Adolphe*, which I had just read with a great deal of pleasure. It made the list of the first ten titles, doubtless puzzling many a high school teacher to whom Constant was not a familiar name. The series grew rapidly and soon became a significant part of NAL's backlist. It was emulated by other paperback publishers, including Penguin. To this day, Signet Classics are a mainstay of NAL's sales, although now that NAL has been bought by Pearson, the series has to compete with the far handsomer Penguin imitations, now also owned by Pearson. Curiously, it did not occur to me at the time that what we had created was an inexpensive version of my father's Pléiade series in France. That thought came to me only much later.

TWO

Pantheon's Second Generation

AFTER MY father's death when I was fifteen, I lost all contact with Pantheon. So I was greatly surprised when, in 1961, I was approached by the Wolffs' successors at Pantheon with an invitation to join them. Pantheon had just been bought by Random House, which realized that at least one full-time editor was needed on the company's tiny staff. I accepted with alacrity and, at the beginning of 1962, as innocent of the problems of publishing as any twenty-six-year-old, I arrived at the Pantheon offices with a great deal of anticipation. These were housed in the triangular skyscraper known as the Little Flatiron Building at Fourth Street and Sixth Avenue. My father's office used to be at the prow of the ship-like edifice and had been kept empty in his homage for many years after his death. The building was shabby, and most of it was occupied by manufacturers, including the premises of an accordion maker and various garment firms. But it was also the site of a number of the country's more interesting publishing houses: New Directions, Pellegrini, and Cuddahy shared our floor, as did the left-wing journal the *Nation* and the Marxist *Monthly Review*.

Since the Wolffs' departure, the firm was being run by the people who had previously been in charge of production and sales — well-intentioned and agreeable men who, however, lacked the editorial skills necessary to maintain the level of books for which the list had become known and that Random expected it to continue publishing. I was sent to work on some marvelous manuscripts, such as Konstantin Paustovsky's *The Story of a Life*, but also a great many second-rate books that had been bought as a result of an excessive reliance on over-enthusiastic readers' reports.

This situation did not last very long. Within a few months, we had moved offices to the ground floor of a small building next to Random House's palatial Villard mansion on Fiftieth Street and Madison, and the new owners were taking a closer look at what they had purchased. Certainly Random House had not lost any money in acquiring the firm. The Pantheon backlist and its very successful children's books were worth much more than the purchase price of the company. Bennett Cerf, in his memoirs, states that the profits from the paperback edition of *Dr. Zhivago* alone had made back the original investment. But the current adult editorial program was indeed a disaster, and within a few months of my arrival, both of my superiors at Pantheon announced they were leaving.

The remaining staff were, for the most part, my age — a handful of young people not much better versed in the politics of publishing than I was. Faced with the departure of our bosses, we rallied together and I suggested to Random House that we be allowed to continue on our own. During my first months at Pantheon, I had been too lowly to meet the directors of the parent company and they seemed a very distant presence. I knew Random House's editor-in-chief, Bennett Cerf, primarily for his column of jokes in the *Saturday Review*, which I had much enjoyed as a youngster, and for his appearance on the television quiz show *What's My Line?* But if Bennett played the clown on television, there was much more to him than the American public perhaps realized. An accomplished writer whose portrait of D. H. Lawrence would have pleased any major literary critic, Bennett had been responsible for bringing James Joyce's *Ulysses* to Random, as well as the work of Gertrude Stein and many other literary stars. His partner, Donald Klopfer, was the traditional quiet counterpart. A close friend of Bennett's (they were famous for having facing desks for many years), he stayed behind the scenes in a self-effacing but crucial role; many people felt he was Random's guiding spirit.

I put it to the partners in charge of the firm that they had very little to lose by allowing us to proceed alone. We had enough titles from our predecessors to tide us over for the coming months. If we failed to find good new books, they could bring the experiment to a close. (At the age of twenty-six, finding another job was not a frightening prospect.) It did not occur to me at the time that handing things over to such young people was highly unusual. Nor did I realize that there was another argument in our favor. Random House, having just bought Alfred A. Knopf, did not want to look as if it were closing down its new literary branches to merge everyone into one firm. Alfred was very concerned that the future of his own imprint might seem in danger if Pantheon was closed.

Apart from such practical considerations, there was a very real idealistic component to the Random House decision to let us carry on. Bennett and Donald looked back on their own beginnings in the business and thought of the gamble we were proposing as a refreshing departure from the current routines. They clearly approved of the intellectual nature of the books we were bringing in, and Donald often spoke of the "touch of class" that they added to Random's output. He saw us as a younger version of what Knopf had accomplished over the years, a renewal of Random's commitment to intellectual and cosmopolitan publishing. Within our first year, they named me editorial director, which was later changed to managing director, and they remained incredibly supportive, giving us, in effect, carte blanche throughout our crucial early years. It was not until much later that the words "profit center" entered my vocabulary. Our role was to publish the best books we could possibly find, although, of course, we also concerned ourselves with whether these books would sell.

Donald in particular was clearly pleased to see Pantheon grow and in later years became my closest adviser and supporter. In the early days, however, he suggested that I turn to Robert Haas for advice. Haas was Random's senior partner, a cultivated and sophisticated publisher from the old school who enjoyed working once again on the kind of books that he had edited in his youth. He was seventy-two when we met, the reverse of my twenty-seven. Despite the disparity in age, I soon discovered we had a similar outlook on publishing. When his own house, Smith & Haas, had merged with Random he brought with him such distinguished French authors as Malraux. He listened quietly as I told him of our hopes and gave me gentle but never intrusive advice. It strikes me now as an extraordinary display of confidence, as well as an indication of how comfortable the Random bosses were in their own roles, that never once was I prevented from taking on any of the many initially unprofitable titles that we published. The closest I remember getting to being reproached was an ever-so-slightly raised eyebrow when I confessed to Donald that I had not yet read the new Mary Renault. (Her historical novels were among the most profitable books we had inherited from the old Pantheon but very far from my own interest.)

As a result of this ideal situation, we were able to spend our time looking for the books that seemed to us to matter the most. We were not so naive as to fail to realize that an occasional best-seller would help, and we spent a great deal of our time on the few promising titles that had been left for us. Thanks to the Wolffs, we were able, in our first year, to publish *The Tin Drum* by Günter Grass, an author who would be awarded the Nobel nearly forty years later. When we presented the book to our sales people, Bennett, who had read the manuscript, was concerned by some of the sexual episodes it contained and expressed his doubts. (Amusingly enough, he did so after asking the only woman in the room to absent herself, lest she be embarrassed by the discussion that was to follow — an indication of the puritanism of those in publishing at that time.) We persuaded Bennett without much difficulty that the manuscript should remain intact, and it is only in recent years that *The Tin Drum* has been objected to in local protests, indicative of the renewed climate of censorship that today plagues so many of our small towns.

Best-selling authors from Pantheon's past such as Renault and Zoë Oldenburg sent us their new manuscripts, which provided a financial underpinning for the more difficult books that we were to bring to the list. I worked with two other people who had been at Pantheon before me. Paula van Doren concentrated on thriving Pantheon backlist authors such as Renault, Alan Watts, and James Morris while Sara Blackburn succeeded in bringing in new writers like Julio Cortázar.

Nineteen sixty-two, the year we started, was not an opportune one for thoughtful, inventive publishing. Even though the McCarthy era had finally ended in 1954, the effects of the years of purging were still powerful. American intellectual life was devastated in this period. It is, I think, a mistake to look at the witch hunts as being concerned primarily with the problems of espionage, internal subversion, and communism. McCarthy had a very clear agenda: to remove New Deal policy makers and intellectuals from positions of influence, both in America and abroad. Despite the fluctuations in the number of "subversives," McCarthy's lists targeted precisely these classic liberals. There is no question that countless communists and fellow travelers suffered greatly as a result of the purges, but McCarthy's political goals were broader: to undo the reforms of the New Deal, a Republican goal since the 1930s. To a large degree he succeeded.

I had come of age during those years and had seen the near-disappearance from American life of dissident and progressive points of view. Though staunchly anticommunist (I grew up on stories of my father's trip to Russia with Gide, which led to the famous *Return from the USSR*, a book detailing the horrors of Stalin's 1930s) I realized how many American voices had been silenced or marginalized. Accordingly, in my first months at Pantheon, I suggested publishing the work of I. F. Stone, the left-wing journalist who was one of the few to speak out against the folly of the McCarthy period.

In later years Stone was recognized as a major influence on American journalism, the mentor to a generation of writers and critics. But when I presented Stone's book, the people at Pantheon who had hired me responded by looking uncomfortable and making excuses about why we could never take on anything so controversial. Around the same time I remember sitting in the offices of the newborn *New York Review of Books*, founded in 1963, seeing the agitation and concern with which Bob Silvers, its editor, discussed the possibility of commissioning Stone to write an article.

Much of the intellectual anticommunism that existed had been heavily subsidized by the CIA (as described in fascinating detail by Frances Stonor Saunders in *The Cultural Cold War*). The resulting climate meant that the number of people working from a liberal viewpoint on American political issues, particularly on foreign policy, was severely limited. The pool of liberal scholars and journalists in the United States from which we could draw was small. Consequently it seemed advantageous to turn to Europe, where intellectual life had not been as badly affected by the battles of the Cold War.

↜↠

I HAD SPENT two years at Cambridge on a graduate grant, coincidentally the Mellon fellowship, working for much of my second year as the first American editor of *Granta*. Our contributors included many contemporaries who were later to become well-known authors and actors in Britain, people like Margaret Drabble, Michael Frayn, Jonathan Spence, John Bird, and Eleanor Bron. Though a student magazine, *Granta* was a sounding board for the whole Cambridge community, and we published many articles by faculty members as well as students, including the architectural critic Rayner Banham and the sociologist Roger Marris. This was a time of great intellectual ferment in Britain. The birth of a new left could already be discerned, developing its ideas in magazines such as *The Universities' and Left Review,* later to become the *New Left Review.* Raymond Williams and Richard Hoggart had just published their first books. Their writing influenced my own thinking and we reviewed them in *Granta.* On returning to the United States, I continued to write for English political magazines and tried to keep abreast of what was happening there. I even received the occasional job offer from British publishers who clearly thought I would enjoy working in London more than in New York.

Looking to Europe made intellectual sense, but it was also a good publishing strategy, since we could find authors in England and Europe who were not already under contract to other, more established American houses and whose books would not require risking too much of Random House's money. Because we were able to publish without worrying whether each new book would make an immediate profit or even show the promise of profit on the author's next work, our criteria for signing a book were straightforward. Above all we were looking for new works that brought the kind of intellectual excitement that American life in the 1950s was lacking. We wanted to find spokesmen for the political outlooks that had been silenced in the McCarthy years, to which I myself felt a strong attraction. As a result we found ourselves in the happy position of admiring people who were often rejected or neglected by others.

After visiting Donald Klopfer one day, the famous Victor Gollancz came to my office, carrying with him the galleys of *The Making of the English Working Class* by the English historian E. P. Thompson. The first evening's reading made me realize that this was the kind of history I had been looking for throughout my university years, both in Britain and the United States. The book was a social and economic history of ordinary people of a kind that had not existed in the 1950s; it was written with extraordinary verve and originality. Gollancz was happy to accept our offer to buy 1,500 copies, and Pantheon's new history list was launched. The book has since sold more than 60,000 copies and is still in print. In Britain, Penguin would honor its paperback edition by choosing it as their thousandth title in the (now defunct) Pelican series. Thompson was followed on our list by other English historians who had until then been relatively unknown in the United States such as Eric Hobsbawm, Christopher Hill, George Rudé, E. H. Carr, Dorothy Thompson, and others.

The excitement we felt at being able to publish this kind of work set us looking for similar books from American authors. Soon after publishing Thompson, we received a doctoral thesis on the history of slavery written by an American Marxist named Eugene Genovese. *The Political Economy of Slavery* had been turned down by twelve university presses because, although its argument was deeply conservative, its methodology was clearly Marxist. Here was a work of extraordinary interest that, like Thompson's, showed how to write history "from the bottom up." I decided to publish the book based solely on my own reactions and instincts, feeling that outside readings would have urged us to follow the university presses in rejecting this controversial manuscript. Along with Genovese's subsequent books, we soon added to the list a number of distinguished Americans such as Herb Gutman, Staughton Lynd, Nathan Huggins, John Dower, Gabriel Kolko, Warren Sussman, Ira Berlin, Richard Fox, and Jackson Lears.

In the end, publishing Genovese proved very difficult. He bitterly attacked his fellow progressive historians, many of whom were on our list. He finally left us when I insisted that we publish Gutman's massive *The Black Family*, over his objections. We had by then published his masterpiece, *Roll, Jordan, Roll*, but I was saddened by Genovese's sectarian excesses and his unwillingness to coexist with others who, after all, shared his basic premises.[17] I did not want our list to represent only one current of thought on any subject — we wanted to show the full range of new work that was developing both in the United States and in Europe.

The British influence on our list was also apparent in literary criticism and what has come to be known as cultural studies. My wife had been an enthusiastic student of F. R. Leavis, and I had heard him lecture at Cambridge. When Leavis wrote his brief attack on C. P. Snow's *Two Cultures*, we hastened to publish it in the United States, to considerable success. We were able to publish Leavis's later work, including the book that he and his wife wrote on Charles Dickens, in which he renounced his previous disdain for the great novelist.

Excited by these early discoveries, I began to make trips to Britain each year. At that time, London was home to dozens of interesting and original publishing houses. I would see seven or eight people a day for the whole of three weeks and feel at the end that I had barely managed to cover the bases. I still thought of Pantheon as a small and impecunious firm, not as part of the Random corporation. Accordingly, we would stay in friends' houses, living the lives of graduate students rather than of fledgling publishers. Some of London's publishers shared this approach too: a few actually had their offices at home, and you had to work your way through a kitchen and past little children to get to a desk full of manuscripts and possibly promising acquisitions.

London was a relatively austere place in those days. When visiting publishing houses with offices in the city such as Routledge, I would walk past blocks of bomb damage, not yet filled with the glittering skyscrapers of the Thatcher era. Nor had British publishing yet been segregated into a few academic publishers and the purely commercial, popular firms on the scene today. Most of the London houses offered a wide range of books, and it was possible to find important works of literature and social science texts just about anywhere you went. Most exciting were the books on politics and history, but there was a great deal of ferment in other areas. I found offerings by the economist Joan Robinson, the political philosopher R. H. Tawney, and the sociologist Tom Bottomore. Richard Titmuss, the chief theoretician of the British welfare state, was another dominant figure. We published his classic book, *The Gift Relationship* (in which blood donations are a symbol for social relations), and as the political climate of the 1960s developed, the *New York Times Book Review* was able to find space for such books on its front page.

As well as buying rights, I began to commission books by young English historians and others. I had long been fascinated by the program of mass observation during World War II, when interviewers fanned out over the country to document the lives of ordinary citizens. I met a young historian called Angus Calder and suggested that he write a book based on these findings. The result, *The People's War*, is still one of the best histories of Britain at that time. Ronald Fraser was another new historian who came to us, this time with the extraordinary oral history of a former Republican mayor of a small Spanish town who had gone underground during the Franco period. *In Hiding* was the first of a series of history books that we were to commission from Fraser, including a major oral history of the civil war, *The Blood of Spain*.

As well as giving me an occasion to recruit authors, the trips to Britain allowed me to meet the numerous young people who were beginning to take over publishing there and who shared my own interests and concerns. The group around Penguin was by far the most exciting. Allen Lane, who was approaching old age, had chosen a young bookseller, Tony Godwin, to be editor-in-chief of Penguin, and Tony had gathered into their simple Georgian building on John Street the highest concentration of talent ever seen in English publishing. Dieter Pevsner, Charles Clark, and Tony Richardson were among the editors who reinvented Penguin and provided British readers with an incredible range of new reading, nonfiction as well as fiction. I came to them with our list of projects and they responded with evident enthusiasm. Their collaboration made it much easier to approach other publishers abroad. We had the beginning of a partnership that went on for many years and one that led, despite Penguin's much larger size, to a large number of shared ventures. Years later, when several of Penguin's key editors left, I was able to persuade my Random House colleagues to back them in setting up a small independent publishing house called Wildwood. The very opposite of what later became Random House

UK, this was designed to be a small, serious house that would distribute Vintage paperbacks and seek out authors and ideas in Britain. Unfortunately, the experiment failed after a few years.

It was through Charles Clark that I first learned about the work of Ronald Laing, a young psychoanalyst and a critic of the medieval practices still employed in British asylums who had written an important academic work with his colleague David Cooper, *Reason and Violence*. But *The Politics of Experience*, which Charles gave me, was something very different. It was a strong polemic on the misunderstanding of madness, an argument for an alternative approach, and a very shocking book, ending with a long description of LSD-induced visions. I hesitated at first, unsure as to how the notoriously conservative American psychoanalytic establishment would respond to such an attack. But Charles wisely told me to set such doubts aside. *The Politics of Experience* became an incredibly popular book, selling half a million copies in paperback, and launching Laing on a meteoric career. Subsequently we published a number of his notable analytical books, including *The Divided Self* and *The Self and Others*.

While Laing is very much in disrepute now, partly because of the way his career ended, much of his work has been accepted by the psychoanalytic profession. His was an important critique, part of an attempt by analysts in Europe and in the United States to reexamine the way schizophrenics were treated. Laing, however, became so well known that oversimplified descriptions of his thesis became part of the counterculture. He was seen as glorifying madness and attributing all mental illness to the evil influence of one's family — an obviously appealing message for the young in the 1960s. Laing helped this process of popularization, becoming something of a guru, and accepting the offers of entrepreneurs to send him on tour throughout the United States, where his lectures drew huge audiences as well as the opprobrium of his colleagues. His writing was increasingly aimed at the mass market. A book of poems called *Knots*, describing the tangles into which relationships can fall, was an enormous success, and Laing began to enjoy the status of the best-selling author, with all the risks that entails. In his later books he repeated what he had said before, and in time his growing reliance on drugs and alcohol began to take its toll, eventually killing him at the age of sixty-two.

The link to Laing and Cooper led us to Juliet Mitchell, an impressive young feminist who sought to reconcile the seeming conflicts between Marxism and Freudian analysis, an effort that she continued in her own subsequent career as an analyst. Mitchell was close to other British feminists such as Ann Oakley and Sheila Rowbotham, and we took on their works, too. Together they helped form a new militant feminism, though their open political engagement ensured their marginalization in the conformist atmosphere that overtook the feminist movement in the United States. In the late 1980s, when I tried to find a university press to reprint Juliet Mitchell's now classic study of psychoanalysis and women, the presses to which we offered the book admitted openly in their rejection letters that the book was too Marxist for them even to consider.

Unfortunately, the collaboration with Penguin that had produced books such as Laing's was under threat. There were early warning signs. The particular affinity with Penguin we had always felt arose from our generational enthusiasm for the intellectual upheaval of the time. But equally important was our shared good fortune: Penguin, like Random, a large corporation, allowed its young people to be in

charge. Their job was not simply to go out and buy the most successful best-sellers of a type published by other houses (though they
did this, too, of course). An important part of the Penguin task was
to continue V. K. Krishna Menon's 1930s vision of an inexpensive
library of engaged nonfiction.

In 1970, Allen Lane sold Penguin to Pearson, one of the major
British conglomerates, and the owners of properties ranging from the
Financial Times to the Buenos Aires Water Company. When Lane
was on his deathbed, Charles Clark and his fellow editors tried to
persuade him to turn Penguin into a public trust, as David Astor had
done with the British Sunday paper the *Observer*, thereby continuing
its independent existence as a nonprofit. Had Lane agreed to this
proposal, the future of British publishing might have been very different. Penguin would have continued to set high standards for
paperback publishing and, by being able to buy books from other
publishers, would have encouraged the rest of the trade to do the
same. It was perhaps too much to expect of Lane, who had always
been a dedicated businessman, and the sale went through. For a
brief period, Pearson turned to a brilliant publisher and author, Peter
Calvocoressi, to be their chief executive. Harper's was to do the same
in the United States, promoting Mel Arnold, the inventor of their
highbrow paperbacks, to president. Both men had come from highly
distinguished small independent firms, Calvocoressi from Chatto &
Windus, Arnold from Beacon Press. I watched their careers with fas-
cination and sadly saw that neither survived the new kind of profit
demands resulting from corporate takeovers.

The same thing happened to the New American Library. NAL's
first corporate takeover took place in 1960, while I was still there.

It became part of Los Angeles Times Mirror, which would go on to buy World Publishing three years later. Bill Targ, one of the few editors who has written his memoirs, had little praise for the new masters, calling them "megalomaniacs and wheeler-dealers" and "market analysts with slide rules up their arses and a power glint in their eyes."[18] NAL's old policies did not last long under this new ownership, and by the time it was bought by Pearson, NAL was simply another popular mass-market line.

I KNEW FROM reading the French papers that a great deal of interesting work being published in France never made its way across the Atlantic. So I began to visit Paris each year in search of possible translations. One of the first books I discovered was Michel Foucault's *History of Madness*. Now required reading in most university social science programs, it had then been available for a number of years in France without attracting the attention of any American critics. I found the book browsing in a Paris bookstore and from the first page I realized this was something of exceptional interest. It appeared on the Pantheon list in 1965 under the title *Madness and Civilization*. We went on to publish all of Foucault's books with great success, though in the first years the U.S. audience was miniscule—evidence that America's intellectual isolation had continued well beyond the McCarthy years. It was hard even to obtain invitations for Foucault from universities, and his reviews in the established journals were largely negative.

Foucault was only one of a number of French authors we added to the list over the following years. Pantheon's authors included scientists such as François Jacob and Octave Mannoni; the social scientists Edgar Morin, Georges Balandier, and Jean Duvigneau; journalists including Claude Julien and André Fontaine, the editors of *Le Monde*, and historians such as Georges Duveaux, Georges Duby, and Moshe Lewin. With the valued help of the Swedish critic Gustaf Bjurström, who had worked with Pantheon in Paris since the 1950s, we also published valuable works of fiction and belles lettres. I had the good fortune to take on Marguerite Duras's work, beginning with *The Lover*, which was the first French novel since *The Mandarins* to become an American best-seller; its success led us to rescue many of her older books from oblivion. (Years later, Duras agreed to have The New Press publish *The North China Lover* as one of its first books, a franker rewriting of her famous memoir.)

As other publishers felt increasing pressure to show profits, even Jean-Paul Sartre found himself rejected by Knopf, which had previously issued most of his work. We gladly took on his later books, including the *War Diaries*, as well as Simone de Beauvoir's *Adieux* — the story of her relationship with Sartre — and paperback editions of many of her earlier titles.

The American response to many of these authors was not at all enthusiastic. Looking back on the long list we so assiduously transposed from Europe, it is striking that, at least initially, we did little better than our predecessors during the war years. We could translate the most interesting and promising of French thinkers, whether in history or in psychoanalysis, but would come up against a brick wall when it came to American readers and reviewers. When, in 1968, Gunnar Myrdal's *Asian Drama* received negative reviews (with the exception of a respectful front page in the *New York Times Book*

Review), I checked the reception given to *The American Dilemma* and his other, earlier works. It was revealing to discover that one of Europe's most important scholars of American society and politics had been initially rejected by the critics, seen as an interfering "Dutch uncle." Considering that Myrdal was the most perceptive critic of the trap into which American society had fallen, a combination of racism and economic inequality, it was perhaps not surprising that Americans refused to read him. Their rejection of his analysis illustrated how difficult it was to change American attitudes. We were no longer dealing with the knee-jerk reactionary thought of the McCarthy period; rather, we were beginning to see the first signs of the neoconservative movement.

I had first met Myrdal when he was invited to give a lecture at a conference in New York in the early 1960s and was impressed by his critique of American social policy. I asked him if he would be willing to write a new book for American readers and he was quick to agree. In later years he would reminisce about a "little brown fellow" who had approached him and asked for a book. (I've never thought of myself as being particularly little or even brown, but compared to Gunnar's massive blond presence, I suppose I was.) The resulting book, *Challenge to Affluence*, began a decades-long collaboration that led to the publication of many of Gunnar's most important works. He was proud of the fact that *Challenge to Affluence* was reported to have been on John F. Kennedy's desk the week he was assassinated. Whether Kennedy paid attention to his argument is something we will never know, but Lyndon Johnson's war on poverty was clearly influenced by the ideas in Gunnar's book.

Thanks to Gunnar, I became friends with his wife, Alva, who had an integral part in international politics, not only as Sweden's ambassador to India but as an intellectual leader for the neutral countries. We published her book *The Game of Disarmament* late in her life; it was part of the work that led to a Nobel Prize. Gunnar's Nobel in economics (shared with Frederick Hayek, a man with whom he totally disagreed) made the Myrdal family unique for having two individual laureates. The rest of the family was equally talented, and we went on to publish several books by their daughter, Sissela Bok, whose *Lying* became a *cause célèbre*, benefiting in particular by being issued at the time of Watergate.

Gunnar also introduced me to his son Jan and urged me to consider publishing his *Report from a Chinese Village*. I was unaware that Jan was famous in Sweden as a leading Maoist; his book of interviews with villagers in the north of Yenan replicated the "Speak Bitterness" campaign that was underway in China to remind the new generation how awful life in nationalist times had been.

When we first received the book in Swedish, our specialized reader approved of its content but suggested that we print it in the smallest possible number, lest it lead readers to a sympathetic view of communist China. After its publication the book was covered as an important event in the *Times*, but a careful reading of their review revealed that the writer had been given access to the CIA's files on Myrdal. Detailed references to conversations he had in Beijing, which couldn't possibly have been known to anyone other than an intelligence service, were sprinkled throughout. Others praised the book highly and it proved to be a terrific success.

We published a number of Jan's books, including an autobiographical novel called *The Diary of a Disloyal European*, which the *Times* hailed as one of the major books of the period. Jan, meanwhile, was distancing himself increasingly from his parents' position, becoming more and more conservative within the Swedish context. Not inconsistent with his Maoism, he became a strong advocate of police power and an opponent of disarmament. He attacked his mother for selling out the Swedes to the Russians in her writings on disarmament and for a while expressed fears that a Russian invasion of Sweden would soon take place. All of this created a curious blend of political and Oedipal conflict, which became increasingly painful to watch as Gunnar and Alva grew older. Jan wrote the first of a trilogy of books about his childhood, attacking his parents mercilessly. Though the books were marvelous memoirs, I felt that publishing them at this point in the life of his parents — Gunnar was close to death — would have been a betrayal on my part, and I urged Jan to wait until his father had died. But vengeance was precisely what Jan had in mind, and he considered my advice to him an attempt at censorship. Our relationship fell apart as a result, and after the books were published to great acclaim in Sweden, another publisher took them on in the United States. In recent years, we have left all of this behind and have renewed our correspondence. But I had learned an unhappy lesson about the dangers that come with publishing a family.

Initially because of the Myrdals, I began to visit Sweden every other year. I found a range of books to translate, thanks in no small part to Gustaf Bjurström. Gustaf had an unerring eye for the best of Swedish literary writing. At his urging we published the novelist Per

Olaf Sundman, the poet Gunnar Ekelov, and the marvelous ten-volume series of Martin Beck mysteries by Per Wahlöö and Maj Sjöwall. These became very popular in the United States, selling well over a million copies in paperback. We also worked closely with Jan's publisher, Lasse Bergstrom of Norstedts, and it was through him that we discovered the work of Ingmar Bergman, whose film scripts we published for many years, including the remarkable *Scenes from a Marriage* and *Fanny and Alexander*. Unfortunately, Bergman's fame was eventually to take him away from us. A Hollywood agent approached him on one of his visits, assuring him that he could easily get a million dollars for his memoirs. Bergstrom was caught having to come up with that sum, or risk losing Bergman. Of course Bergman's memoir never earned anything like that amount, but his expectation of such a vast advance forced us to stand aside.

As the years progressed, Pantheon found partners in Germany, Italy, and post-Franco Spain. The Frankfurt Book Fair gave us the opportunity to bring our colleagues together not only to compare notes but to commission books jointly. The editorial staff of Pantheon, myself included, was relatively young and untried. We had neither the experience nor the acquaintances needed for the broad range of fields in which we were interested. Agents and authors were more likely to go to the better established parts of the Random group than to come to us. Of course we could have offset this by offering large amounts of money for new books, outbidding Random and Knopf. But I knew the kinds of titles we were interested in would not sell huge numbers and that it would be foolish to get involved in expensive bidding wars. Looking overseas was a better alternative, and by working in unison with our European partners we were able to minimize the risks to each individual firm. Of equal importance was the conviction that we were participating in a common enterprise of shared cultural and political value.

✺

AS THE 1960s came to a close, challenging work that had previously been the province primarily of Europe began to appear in the United States, and we were able to offer something in exchange to our new European partners. Books by Noam Chomsky and Studs Terkel were translated into every major European language. We also sought to collaborate with our colleagues in creating new titles that we could publish together. Working with the publishers who had translated Jan Myrdal's *Report from a Chinese Village*, we commissioned a series of analogous titles from villages throughout the world that documented the enormous social changes taking place among ordinary people, in their own words.

We looked to a wide variety of authors, some of them social scientists, others novelists, to go to small villages in their own countries, or in those countries' former colonies, and see if they could capture the voices of people as they sought to understand and explain their own experience. The series had broad appeal throughout the world, and the books were widely translated. They also formed a fascinating parallel to the new kind of history books that we were publishing, books that told what had happened in the past to ordinary people as the village books looked at the present.

A dozen volumes from various countries were published in the series; colleagues in half a dozen countries shared the task of commissioning books. We all wanted to overcome the usual mercantilist constraints on publishing. The idea that publishers should work together only to sell work at a profit seemed banal and inappropriate. As time passed, an international partnership was developed with many publishers throughout the world, Penguin chief among them. Tony Godwin commissioned Ronald Blythe to write *Akenfield*, the very successful British component of the series, and went on to publish an English edition of Studs Terkel's books and many of the other volumes that we had commissioned.

It was this project that led me to what became my longest and closest association with any author during my years at Pantheon, and beyond. Looking for authors who could write the equivalent of Myrdal's book about the United States, my thoughts turned to Studs Terkel, the Chicago disc jockey whose daily program of music and interviews was well known there. His interviews, which I used to read in the magazine published by his station, WFMT, were extraordinarily sharp and effective. Through a mutual friend, the English actress Eleanor Bron (who was playing in Chicago with Second City at the time), I met Studs and discovered that, although he was now broadcasting on a small FM station, he had once been one of the great stars of the "Chicago school of television." With David Garroway, he had pioneered a series of spontaneous broadcasts, live and unscripted, in which he and a group of associates created a popular hangout called Studs's Place.

Studs had started out as a stage, television, and radio actor, having graduated from the University of Chicago law school at the height of the Depression, when jobs for lawyers were scarce and the WPA (Work Projects Administration) was offering theater as an exciting alternative. He had been involved in a number of progressive causes, including the Henry Wallace campaign of 1948, and had become the bête noire of the *Chicago Tribune* and its archreactionary publisher, the famous Colonel Robert McCormick. So opposed was that paper to Studs that it would not even list his radio program in its pages. Other pressures had helped to force Studs off television and had come close to ending a promising career.

Studs was tempted by the idea of writing an oral history and amused that a New Yorker might think of a Chicago neighborhood as a possible village. Studs's first book, *Division Street*, was a revelation. By tracing the lives of ordinary Chicago residents, he described the dramatic changes a cross-section of seemingly unremarkable people experienced. Many people, both white and black, had come to Chicago from Appalachia and the deep South and theirs was the history of the great post-World War II migration that had transformed millions of lives. The press throughout the country praised the way Studs had captured the voices of the people he interviewed, without condescension and with the respect that would mark all his books. Years later I discovered that what we had embarked on was very similar to the interviews that the WPA had sponsored during the 1930s, where distinguished writers interviewed Americans about their jobs and their backgrounds. It was the first time since then that such an oral history had been written and it became an immediate best-seller.

After its initial success, I suggested to Studs that he write an oral history of the 1930s, since many of those who had lived through that period could still be interviewed. *Hard Times* did even better than the first book and by the time we published *"The Good War,"* the his-

tory of America's experience during World War II, we had first printings of 100,000 copies. *Working: People Talk About What They Do
All Day and How They Feel About What They Do* was the most popular of Studs's books, selling well over a million copies in various
paperback editions; it was then used as a textbook in college and
high school courses throughout the country. Typical of Studs, when
a small Southern town protested the foul but accurate language that
he quoted in *Working*, he chose to go down to address a town meeting and discuss the issue with the people involved. He did not want
to rely on our sending out the usual press release in defense of the
First Amendment, he wanted to talk to the people himself and see
exactly what it was they objected to. It would be nice to be able to
report that this intervention succeeded in persuading them. But in
this case, the effort was as worthy as any success might have been.

＋〜＋

IT WAS CLEAR in the early 1960s that action would precede words
in a number of crucial areas. The growth of the civil rights movement helped create a massive audience for writing on racial issues,
but evidently those who demonstrated at Selma, Alabama, and elsewhere did not need our books to tell them what was wrong. Books
on this subject in time became important in persuading a white
readership of the need for change and in suggesting new approaches
and tactics. But it was African-American activists who led the way
and we who followed.

Some of the very first books we commissioned dealt with issues
of race including a great early work on black history. I approached

a young historian at Princeton, James MacPherson, to edit a collection of texts by African Americans on their experiences during the Civil War. (The book's title, *The Negro's Civil War*, indicates how early on in the discussion of race it was published.) MacPherson became one of the most distinguished historians of the Civil War. We also commissioned a number of books on the law and race, including work by the distinguished African-American jurors Robert Carter and Loren Miller, as well as titles telling what was happening in the South. One such, *Southern Justice*, edited by Leon Friedman, gathered the writings of many of the young lawyers who had volunteered to help the civil rights movement in the South, some of whom later published important books about racism. One of these was Paul Chevigny, whose definitive study of police brutality we have since published at The New Press. Joel Kovel, like Chevigny, an old schoolmate, attempted a psychoanalytical approach to racism, and his *White Racism*, a psycho-history, won great praise.

In addition to publishing books on the question of race itself, we felt a strong responsibility to cover the South and its history. Starting with Pat Watters, Les Dunbar, Bill Ferris, and others, we published a series of distinguished southern white liberals who had courageously carried on the struggle well before Northerners had become familiar with the issues involved. James Loewen, a young professor at Tougaloo, worked with a group of his associates to put together the first high school textbook of Mississippi history that countered the existing overtly racist texts. These books, widely assigned in the state, dealt with the origins of the Ku Klux Klan in a positive fashion and neglected much of Mississippi's fascinating and diverse history. Loewen and his colleagues worked hard to put together an alternative text that they hoped would be used in the state's schools. Not surprisingly, the textbook publishers they approached turned the book down. Finally, they came to us and I agreed to take the project on, provided we could get it by our colleagues at Random House.

The Random House textbook people violently opposed its publication. Random House's school division, Singer, was among its least distinguished acquisitions — despite its employment of Toni Morrison as an editor for a brief period. Mississippi was one of the few states sufficiently behind in its standards to have been a steady purchaser of Random's textbooks, and those in charge of Singer reasonably feared that their competitors would be quick to point out our publication. I joked with Bob Bernstein, Random's CEO, that we should publish the book under the rubric "Pantheon Books, a Division of D. C. Heath," a rival textbook firm. But Bob indicated that he was willing to back us with a decision that could easily cost Random millions of dollars in sales. The resulting book, *Mississippi, Conflict and Change*, won high praise. It was not adopted by the Mississippi public schools, though Catholic schools and some independent schools did take it on. The NAACP Legal Defense Fund in Jackson, Mississippi, led by Melvyn Leventhal, offered to contest the state's refusal to allow public purchases of the textbook, and the case was finally heard by the U.S. District Court for the Northern District of Mississippi. Arguing with great effectiveness that the schools could not be meaningfully desegregated if the material that they taught was still racist, Frank R. Parker won the case. By then, however, Reagan was in office and the possibilities of enforcing the decision were negligible. Our sales people discovered that when they called the Mississippi school districts to pitch the book, the officials would simply hang up on them. The book remained in print for several years, but never had the impact it clearly deserved.

The problems of race and poverty were intertwined, and we were immersed in trying to find ways of dealing with both issues. Richard Cloward and Frances Fox Piven were activists and intellectuals who made such connections. They had been deeply involved in the protests that had helped to bring about Lyndon Johnson's social policy. Their first book, *Regulating the Poor* (1971), proved to be a phenomenon in the nation's universities, selling over half a million copies and helping to form the curriculum of countless political science and sociology courses. This was one of the rare books in which thought and action were intimately tied together.

In 1970, a Boston political scientist, William Ryan, wrote a devastating critique of Daniel Moynihan's book on race and family for the *Nation*. On the advice of the magazine's editor at the time, Carey McWilliams, we wrote to Ryan asking if he wanted to expand the article. *Blaming the Victim* was the well-chosen title of the book that resulted; it also sold more than half a million copies. Sales of this kind for serious political work had not been seen since the war years and marked a breakthrough in American reading habits. Our colleagues at Random House were enjoying similar success with books on the Vietnam War and the civil rights movement. Books by black leaders such as Eldridge Cleaver and Malcolm X achieved extraordinary sales, showing how much public opinion had changed since the publication of Myrdal's book in the 1940s.

We also worked very hard to forge a link with Ralph Nader and his various organizations. Ralph's first book, *Unsafe at Any Speed*, a criticism of standards of automobile safety, made him a prominent critic of American industry. Wielding an organizational skill that few had credited him with, Ralph built a series of groups in Washington that dealt with specific issues such as automobile safety, the environment, and consumer advocacy. He also helped to organize a network of PIRGs, public interest research groups, in every major city.

Nader's book with Pantheon was one of his best. Published in 1988 and written with his colleague John Richardson, *The Big Boys* was a series of portraits of the heads of large corporations, based on interviews with the executives themselves. Ralph was able to extract extraordinarily frank accounts from the heads of some of the larger firms and in earlier, more favorable times, the book would surely have been an enormous success. But in the 1980s the climate had changed, and the right could attack Nader on principle, without having to make much of a case. When *The Big Boys* was finally published, it met with the kind of stifled-yawn reviews that are intended to kill a book.

(It is extremely difficult to launch a public discussion critical of large corporations. With the exceptions of the tobacco industry and gun manufacturers, which are a clear and present danger to public health, most large industries have managed to keep themselves insulated against outside criticism. As a whole the press does not feature detailed investigations of corporate policies in its business pages. Ironically, it is the *Wall Street Journal*, whose editorial pages had discouraged people from talking to Nader when he was researching *The Big Boys*, that has been the most distinguished exception to this overall rule. But with the tens of thousands of books on business being published every year, it is remarkable how

few feature a careful look at what is really going on, important as
this might be for would-be investors, not to speak of workers in the
industries themselves or the citizenry as a whole.)

Until the escalation of the Vietnam War in the late 1960s, books
on foreign policy were rarely published. So limited was the interest in Cold War foreign affairs that the CIA had to covertly subsidize the publication of hundreds of books pushing the government
line. Contrary to the federal laws governing its activities, these
books, ostensibly published only for foreign audiences, naturally
found their way into the American market. Indeed, as with much
of American propaganda during this period, the domestic reader
was probably the intended audience from the beginning. During
the congressional hearings about the CIA's activities in the United
States in the 1960s, hundreds of titles made public. (Many of them
were published by Praeger, a firm started by a young Austrian émi-
gré who had originally worked with the American occupying forces
in his own country.) Such publications had not been necessary during the previous era. Books published during World War II uniformly backed American foreign policy. There was no formal
censorship and, I suspect, no informal pressure. Publishers interested in foreign policy, like Cass Canfield of Harper's, belonged to
the establishment and generally agreed with the state department.
During World War II, for instance, I can think of no book that was
published that discussed the Holocaust or criticized American foreign policy toward the Jews or others who were being exterminated.
As in Hollywood, where not a single film even mentioning these
issues appeared until well after the war, publishing was extraordinarily silent.

Likewise during the early Cold War years, very little was published, except by a few communist publishers, that discussed the changes taking place in Eastern Europe and Latin America. It was only in the 1960s that the thaw began to affect American intellectual life as well as American publishing. We first published books about communist China. That area of the world was still very much a blank on the map of the American media, and the China lobby had been extraordinarily successful in persuading most Americans that the nationalist regime should have stayed in power and was worthy of support.

We would publish much more on China and Japan in the coming years, including John Dower's *War Without Mercy* and, at The New Press, his magisterial *Embracing Defeat*, which won the 1999 Bancroft Prize, the Pulitzer Prize, and the National Book Award. At first, our books on China focused on trying to give a more accurate picture of the Chinese revolution than that provided by the State Department and the China lobby. But as time passed, our books became more critical of China's new policies. In them was the first realistic description of the cultural revolution and the growth of a corrupt new class in Chinese society. I was able to travel twice to China and there met a new generation of impressive writers and critics. The most important was Liu Binyan, a courageous journalist whose exposés of governmental corruption had landed him in jail. When I first met him, he was still under police guard but he spoke to me frankly and forcibly. We signed him up to write several books.

In time, we were to publish as much on Latin America as on Asia. Eduardo Galeano's trilogy, *The Memory of Fire*, made an enormous impact, as did Cortázar's novels. But the most dramatic books dealt with Chile, about which we published a small book by Regis Debray and Salvador Allende, debating the future of Chile's revolution. I asked Chile's American ambassador, Orlando Letelier, to write an introduction and met with him in his Washington embassy at the start of the Nixon administration. I asked him if he thought that Washington would leave his government alone. Unaware of Kissinger's plots, he replied that Washington seemed friendly and speculated that perhaps Nixon was following the policies that had led him to establish relations with China. Soon thereafter, Allende was killed in a coup and Letelier himself was later assassinated in Washington by the DINA, Chile's secret police. I was glad that at least we were able to publish the exposé of these events. *Assassination on Embassy Row* by John Dinges and Saul Landau was instrumental in eventually bringing Letelier's murderers to justice.

We were late in publishing books on the Vietnam War. I was overoptimistic in thinking that the war was such a disaster that it could not continue. After a few years, I realized how foolish these expectations were. Other publishers were more realistic, and a vast number of books on Vietnam and Southeast Asia appeared from firms of all sizes. Finally, we found the book that I felt placed the opposition to the war in Vietnam in the most telling context, Noam Chomsky's *American Power and the New Mandarins*. We continued to publish Chomsky for many years and his books were among the most important and satisfying on our list.

As the rejection of America's Cold War policies became more widely accepted, we found ourselves publishing some of the people who had been instrumental in formulating American policies but who had become intensely critical of the way these played out; issuing this work was also a sign of our new proximity to the mainstream. George Kennan had written an impressive critique of American nuclear policy that I persuaded him to turn into a short book, *The Nuclear Delusion*. We published several more of his books in our last years at Pantheon, and they were among our most successful titles. At the same time, I suggested to former secretary of defense Robert McNamara that he write the first of what proved to be a series of books analyzing the mistakes of the Vietnam War. We also went back to Senator J. William Fulbright, whose *Arrogance of Power* had been one of Random House's most outstanding contributions to the Vietnam debate, and asked him to write a book of his reflections on American policy of the past decade.[19] These elder statesmen were greeted with the respect they had earned, and their books sold remarkably well.

LOOKING THROUGH other catalogs from the 1960s and 1970s reminded me that Pantheon was not alone in publishing books on political issues. Even houses representing the most stolid of establishment values, such as Harper's, published widely on the issues of racial and social inequality. A clear consensus from the center to the left dominated American publishing. Pantheon stood out for its cosmopolitanism — the degree to which it looked outside the United States for new and often dissenting ideas. But in general terms, our books were very much in line with the output of other publishers. Indeed, in certain fields, there were publishers well to our left. These included the long-established Marxist publishers such as Monthly Review but also those representing the cultural and sexual left, like Barney Rosset's Grove Press. (As we have seen in the past year, it was the sexual revolution that turned out to have the longest-lasting power and the broadest mass support. The Republicans since Ronald Reagan may have undone many of the economic reforms that the Democrats had put into place from the New Deal on, but even Kenneth Starr and his colleagues were unable to mobilize public opinion behind their attempt to negate the sexual revolution.)

Michael Korda's entertaining and well-received memoir of much of this period, *Another Life*, presents an interesting snapshot of the ways publishing has changed over the past four decades and, perhaps unwittingly, endorses many of those changes. Korda, who has been Simon & Schuster's chief editor for many years, began his career at the firm in 1958. Simon & Schuster's list in those days was a mixture of popular books — including a highly profitable line in crossword puzzles — and more demanding titles such as the multi-volume *Story of Civilization* written by Will and Ariel Durant.[20] Korda pokes gentle fun at Max Schuster, who started out as an editor of an automotive trade magazine, and his partner Dick Simon, a former piano salesman. Korda was from the renowned Hungarian filmmaking family and, fresh from Oxford, he looked down on these middle-class Jews and their pretensions to serve the world of culture. He writes that Schuster's wall was covered with photographs of his famous authors, a common enough practice, but notes that people like the art historian Bernard Berenson appeared surprised at being captured on film with Schuster and his wife, perhaps confused about who they were or why they were there. When Schuster started in publishing, Korda writes, vulgarity was still frowned upon. Bad taste frightened publishers. Bennett Cerf might flutter around the edges of show business, a Broadway groupie, joke anthologist, and panel member on *What's My Line?*, but when it came to his publishing persona, he expected to be taken seriously and worried about books "in bad taste." Max's ambition as a publisher was to load the S & S list with works of philosophy, history, and great literature, and he put his ears back and shied at the idea of anything that might be in bad taste carrying his name.[21]

But the fact remains that Simon & Schuster published serious books over a wide range of subjects in this period, in stark contrast to what they publish today. Although most of these titles are not mentioned in Korda's memoir, it is worth noting that in 1960 the firm published Bertrand Russell's *Sense in Nuclear Warfare* in one of their new paperback formats: hardly a book of assured popularity. Also on the list was J. Robert Oppenheimer's *The Open Mind* and William Shirer's *The Rise and Fall of the Third Reich*. Random House, too, had a respectable mix that year, including John Strachey's *The End of Empire* and Wylie Sypher's *Rococo to Cubism in Art and Literature* — again, titles that certainly would not appear in their current catalogs.

The Harper's list from 1960 is even more surprising. Today, one thinks of HarperCollins as a publisher of extremely commercial titles as well as how-to and entertainment books. A look at Harper's forty years ago couldn't provide a more dazzling contrast. While their fiction list was not particularly distinguished, the number of interesting books on history and politics is quite extraordinary. Twenty-eight titles are listed for the spring of 1960, among them Robert Heilbroner's *The Future As History* and W. W. Rostow's *The*

United States in the World Arena. Harper's also launched the Harper Torch Books (now all erased from the Harper's backlist), which ranged from a series on religion including Nicholas Berdyaev's *The Destiny of Man* to Arnold Kettle's two-volume Marxist introduction to the English novel.

These titles were issued at a time when the intellectual awakening of the late 1960s, spurred on by the opposition to the Vietnam War and the debate around domestic issues, had yet to happen. America was still a very quiet place, intellectually speaking. The books, therefore, were not aimed at a clearly perceived intellectual and academic audience. Rather than benefiting from change, this list helped bring it about.

By 1970, we can see the degree to which the overall intellectual scene had been altered, partly by previous publishing efforts. Simon & Schuster's 1970 spring list includes *Do It!* by Jerry Rubin, and Yoko Ono's *Grapefruit* as well as Derek Bok's and John Dunlop's *Labor and the American Community*. The Random House list combines *I Know Why the Caged Bird Sings* by Maya Angelou with W. H. Auden's translation of *The Elder Edda*, the anthropologist Vincent Crapanzano's *The Fifth World of Enoch Maloney*, and William Douglas's *Points of Rebellion*. The Harper list includes Alexander Bickel's book on the Supreme Court; Hugh Thomas's book on the history of Cuba; a groundbreaking book on Vietnam by Paul Mus and John McAlister, *The Vietnamese and Their Revolution*; Kenneth Clark's *Civilisation*; and Todd Gitlin's early book on the poor whites of Chicago, *Uptown*.

The people who were responsible for these books were not a bunch of wild-eyed radicals determined to spread their vision throughout the land, though a number of editors in the major houses did have strong political commitments. Harper's was still very much the pillar of the establishment that it had always been. The house, known for its links to the government and to the Ivy League, was run by distinguished and cautious men. But the people who ran Harper's were good publishers, capable of responding to the widespread radicalism of the day.

Dozens of publishers, most of which have since disappeared (as independent houses), were producing intellectually important books. Some, like McGraw-Hill, which published great authors like Vladimir Nabokov, have turned to business and technical books. Others, like Schocken, Dutton, or Quadrangle, have been subsumed into the larger corporate groups and deprived of any meaningful identity. Still others, such as John Day and McDowell Obolensky, have joined the annals of history, part of a now largely forgotten past.

The changes that took place at Harper's can be traced primarily to its new owners. When Rupert Murdoch took over the firm in 1987, it moved very quickly in the direction it has been going ever since, concentrating on the most commercial books, particularly those that can be linked to Murdoch's entertainment holdings. The political content of the list also changed, so that instead of books by the Kennedys and other liberals, the house now took on the memoirs of Colonel Oliver North and Newt Gingrich. Murdoch brought in his own people from Britain to replace those who had long been associated with the firm.

Developments at Simon & Schuster were more complex and occurred over a longer period of time. Korda, on the evidence of his memoir, is curiously ambivalent about these changes. With a few distinguished exceptions, such as Graham Greene, an old family friend and a childhood idol, and the Texas novelist Larry McMurtry, Korda was concerned with the authors of highly commercial best-sellers, such as Harold Robbins, Irving Wallace, and Jacqueline Susann. He subsequently took on political best-sellers by authors Richard Nixon and (putatively) Ronald Reagan.

Korda describes these authors, on which the firm's fortunes were increasingly to rely, with remarkable disdain. They are demanding, their clothing is vulgar, they do not know the right places in London at which to order custom-made shoes, or the appropriate restaurants at which to eat — subjects on which Korda is very well informed. At the same time, he describes their books as the unavoidable wave of the future as publishing becomes increasingly tied to the entertainment industry, and the styles and values of Hollywood become dominant. Celebrity books are the titles that will make or break firms and Korda, with his boss, Richard Snyder, are determined that it will be the former.

In time Simon & Schuster was bought by Viacom, owners of Paramount Pictures, and for a brief while it was even renamed Paramount Books. While Korda is frank in describing the economic pressures of these changes, he is nonetheless firmly wedded to the assumption that these are the books on which publishing should focus, and he is proud of his successes with them, if not of his associations with their authors. At one point, he allows himself a very harsh judgment about Harold Robbins, one of his first successful commercial authors. Robbins had written a promising first literary work in the manner of proletarian novels of the 1930s, and had even been published by Knopf.

> Like most people who have sold out, Robbins was bitter about having done it and felt that he had sold out for too little. In interviews he always sounded cocky and quick to defend his books against the critics, but the truth was that he despised his readers and despised himself for catering to them.[22]

It seems that in today's publishing it is only authors who despise themselves for selling out. Publishers merely anticipate inevitable trends.

THREE

Fixing the Bottom Line

IN RETROSPECT, it is surprising that while our optimistic publishing efforts were closely geared to the rapidly changing society in which we lived, we were oblivious to the developments occurring inside the corporation that employed us. In 1965, Random House was bought by the giant electronics empire RCA, and it was not long before the bookkeeping expectations that were widespread elsewhere in publishing began to be felt in Pantheon. The profits from our successful children's books were no longer to be attributed to us, nor were the sales of our university textbooks. Since trade publishing was known to work with initially unprofitable titles, we all depended on income from lines with better margins such as these. In time, the rules were changed again and each book was expected to make a sufficient contribution both to overhead and to profit.

Wall Street was abuzz with expectations of synergy. It was thought that RCA would move into the new business of teaching machines, an early and failed version of what computers were later to achieve. Random's school textbooks would then nourish this effort, to the profit of all. But the purchase had not been thought out carefully, and RCA had not realized that Random's textbooks were among the weakest titles it published. Likewise, the antitrust laws at the time discouraged intracorporate agreements of this sort. Random was not what RCA expected, any more than Henry Holt had been what CBS expected or what Raytheon had desired in the other contemporary major mergers. All of these finally fell apart within a few years of each other, leaving the publishing houses like beached whales, unsure of who would rescue them.

There had been years when Pantheon earned only a small amount but, as Bennett Cerf and Donald Klopfer's successor Bob Bernstein was often to insist, at no time did we lose any money out of pocket. That is, Pantheon covered its own costs even if it did not always contribute the required amount to Random's expenditures, a sum of which we were never informed and could not negotiate. To make matters worse, these charges were not simply a percentage of the overall expenditures, which were skyrocketing, but also included nonexistent services and inequitable percentages. Bernstein recently stated that Pantheon did not "need the huge sales overhead Random House maintained to sell its juvenile list and other mass merchandise books," for which it was charged.[23] For years I tried in vain to find out what these expenses were. It was only as I was about to leave that a friendly accountant confessed to me how exaggerated the overbillings had been. In our last days at Pantheon I discovered that the warehouse charged more to ship our books than the books of other houses in the Random group because, it was claimed, our books more often sold in single copies — which was never proved. I discovered that I had been billed over the years for a car, even though I do not drive. I had often suggested that we move out of the expensive Random House building, and when we acquired Schocken, we could easily have gone to their shabbier premises on Cooper Square. But the corporation preferred to keep those offices empty for years rather than allow a logical move that would have saved everyone money.

With the success of Studs's books and other best-sellers, it became clear that while Pantheon would not be immensely profitable, it would not lose Random any money. The books that had once seemed adventurous and difficult intellectual works were ending up on university reading lists. The backlist sold in a higher proportion every year, covering most of our costs. Overall, backlist sales, a crucial index for any serious publisher, grew steadily to 50 percent. By 1990, Pantheon sales were nearly $20 million annually.

But as the pressures on Pantheon for growth and profit increased, it became clear that the weightier titles on the list would never sell enough to meet the budgetary goals imposed on us. Even though the sales of Pantheon's political books in the 1980s were nowhere near as successful as they were in the 1960s and 1970s, we had ever more books on university course lists. And a few critiques of Reagan did manage to break through the Teflon Curtain. Bob Lekachman was one of the first trenchant critics with *Greed Is Not Enough: Reaganomics,* which made the *Times* best-seller list. In spite of our sales team's certainty that any attack on Reagan was foredoomed, Mark Green's collection *Reagan's Reign of Error* sold over 100,000 copies, showing that a far greater anti-Reagan audience existed than was commonly assumed. Still, the increasingly frequent budget reviews, familiar to anyone who has worked in corporate America, forced me to look for books that would sell in greater quantities and at higher prices. I found more and more of my time was being spent on acquiring books for the sole purpose of turnover, books which, for the most part, could have been published far more successfully by others in Random House. Our European colleagues watched this change in our catalog with growing puzzlement. Their houses published cookbooks and books on decorating as well, but they were produced by special departments, expert in their fields. The editors in charge of the more intellectual aspects of those companies' output had no business dabbling in other areas.

Random conducted a study that showed that none of its components made money from the glossy books bought from packagers here and abroad. In the desperate search for higher income, we were all spinning our wheels, very expensively. The logic of the profit center began to be counterproductive. The need for each entity to achieve an annual increase in sales and profit forced every part of the publishing house to duplicate the other's efforts and to compete for the most lucrative titles. Like many other publishers, Random had launched specific lines for more popular books. The Villard imprint was created to produce more popular fiction that neither Random nor Knopf was interested in. (I remember Alfred Knopf's instant refusal of *The Scarsdale Diet*, a book written by his own doctor, which became one of the most popular diet books of all time. There was no question in Alfred's mind that the book should not appear on the Knopf list, and he did not even bother to suggest to the author that he turn to another part of Random House. His decision was not considered unusual or unwise then.)

The decision by RCA to sell off Random in 1980 left the publishing house in a very awkward position. A number of major publishers had gone on the market at roughly the same time, and their owners were having great difficulty finding new purchasers. Random was now too large to be bought by any individual buyer, but issuing stocks afresh would be complicated and risky. The other conglomerates were backing off from the buying spree they had been on in past years for much the same reasons that had led RCA to unload Random. There were no obvious purchasers in sight. Even the low asking price of $60 million seemed beyond anyone's interest.

Enormous was the relief of Bernstein and his colleagues when S. I. Newhouse approached them. Newhouse, like Rupert Murdoch, was one of a handful of multibillionaire media owners. He and his brother Donald had inherited a chain of newspapers from their father that were immensely profitable, although of little editorial merit. Through dailies such as the *Staten Island Advance* and the Newark *Star-Ledger*, they had amassed a fortune that allowed them to purchase the Condé Nast magazine dynasty as well as a network of valuable cable television stations. The brothers owned it all outright, with no shareholders to report to and no one with whom they had to share their profits. They were said to be worth at least $10 billion.

Si, as he is called, was already a controversial figure of great renown. Famed for his art collection, which he bought with the advice and counsel of Alex Lieberman, the editorial director of

Vogue, he seemed in every respect the model of an intellectual and sophisticated billionaire. He reportedly once spent $17 million on a Jasper Johns without a moment's hesitation and sold it later at a loss of $10 million, apparently with the same equanimity.

As it happened, I had known Newhouse and his wife Victoria through other channels — I had once been involved in deciding whether Victoria's small, nonprofit architectural publishing house deserved an NEA grant. It was in a social rather than a business context that Si asked me if I thought it would be worth his while to buy Random. I answered that if he wanted to add to his collection the most prestigious of the American publishing groups, it was a unique opportunity. But, I added (perhaps foolishly), if his interest was to make more money than he could in his other holdings, then he should pass up the opportunity. He smiled politely.

Newhouse took over Random with the firmest of assurances: he emphasized that he had bought us for our intellectual and cultural merit. He insisted he had no intention of trying to run a publishing house. He was very happy with the employees in place, and intended to allow us to continue what we were already doing so well, only with greater resources. He would subsequently make precisely the same promise when he bought the *New Yorker* magazine. That promise was broken within a year. The commitment made to Random House took longer to dispose of.

In retrospect, it is clear that all of us listened to Newhouse's assurances with a mixture of gullibility and innocence. Of course we wanted to believe in the idea of a fairy godfather whose $10 billion wand would wave away any difficulties we might face. To my knowledge, none of us thought to ask colleagues in Newhouse's other holdings how he had run their businesses and at what cost. Had we done so, we would have discovered a clear and alarming pattern.

When Newhouse took over Condé Nast, a series of changes were put into place, magazine by magazine. In every case, hitherto successful publications were deemed to be addressed to too small an audience and were thus insufficiently profitable. Profits that had been considered acceptable in the past, Newhouse and his managers insisted, were only a fraction of what they could be. *Vogue* was no longer to appeal to elite concepts of style but was to address a larger, more popular audience. This change in itself would be lamented by only a small number of readers. Far more telling would be the changes to the magazine aimed at boosting advertising revenue. New design so blurred the line between editorial and advertising pages that only the most discerning reader could tell one from the other. And *Vogue* stopped paying for trips taken by its travel writers. These were to be covered by the airlines and others — in return, of course, for favorable mentions.

As time passed, magazines ranging from *Mademoiselle* to the *New Yorker* would undergo these changes. In the latter case, a magazine that had prided, indeed defined, itself by the division between advertisements and content was transformed under Newhouse into one that devoted specific issues to advertiser-driven themes such as fashion so as to assure new and highly profitable advertising packages.

It is only in retrospect that the inevitability of this pattern emerged, though we ought to have been able to identify it at the start. While initially claiming that he would leave editorial decisions alone, Newhouse soon made changes at Random House that moved it in a far more commercial direction. Random's profitable college department (as opposed to its weak school line) was sold off early in the game; Newhouse was so eager to get rid of it that he was willing to sell it for half of what it subsequently fetched when it was resold. This money was used to buy one of America's most commercial firms, Crown Books, which promised big sales at the bottom of the market. But Crown turned out to have been far less profitable than the Newhouse accountants predicted. In these as in many other transactions, it was clear that the desire to make more money overrode the normal counsels of caution and care. Vast amounts were lost in selling and buying parts of Random House, as money was later lost on the *New Yorker* and other journals, on the general assumption that larger circulation was the sure path to higher profit.

Despite his early promises of editorial independence, Newhouse soon became personally involved in acquiring titles. He insisted that Random House pay a huge advance to Donald Trump, the New York real estate speculator whose adventures and many failures are still the butt of jokes in tabloid articles. Newhouse, who spoke with great admiration about his fellow tycoons profiled on the television program *Lifestyles of the Rich and Famous*, was as attracted to glitz as a moth to a flame. He arranged for huge advances to be paid to figures who clearly had very little to say in public but whose names were supposed to attract the curious masses. For example, Nancy Reagan was paid $3 million for her memoirs, a sum that went largely unearned and that inspired one wit to ask whether it was an advance against royalties or a tip for services rendered by the Reagans to the very rich. Newhouse also saw to it that Random House signed up a book by his old friend and McCarthy sidekick, Roy Cohn. (The book was assigned to Random's editorial director, Jason Epstein, but Cohn died before it was finished.)

Murdoch at HarperCollins would encourage his editors to pay similar advances, often to equally conservative recipients. The thriller writer Jeffrey Archer, then head of Britain's Conservative Party, received $35 million in advances for three novels that crashed so resoundingly that the finances of the American branch of HarperCollins were severely shaken. In time, Newhouse would institutionalize a system within Random House that maximized these follies: he allowed the heads of the various publishing houses within Random to bid against each other, rather than in concert, as before. As a result of such competition, books like Colin Powell's memoirs received multimillion-dollar advances, far higher than would have otherwise been the case.

Bob Bernstein became ever more uncomfortable with these new and extravagant ways. Bernstein had risen through the commercial side of the firm, having initially been employed as sales manager. He proved to be a brilliant businessman, but he also realized how important it was to have a decentralized firm run by its editors rather than its accountants. When confronted with publishing decisions that involved ethical considerations, he invariably landed on the right side. At bottom, he was a very committed man, with a special interest in issues of human rights. He appreciated the social responsibilities of a major publisher like Random House, both within America and on the world stage.

Random House's worth was steadily increasing because of Newhouse's investments and a number of very successful purchases, particularly of paperback lines, that Bernstein engineered. A firm that had been bought for $60 million in 1980 was worth over $800 million by 1990. But this spectacular fifteenfold growth in the value of its assets was not enough for Newhouse. He wanted more annual profit, and Random House, though in the black, failed to show such increases. Here again, because Newhouse's figures were kept secret, we did not know that part of his concern resulted from his extravagant spending on the Condé Nast magazines, which had placed nine of eleven titles in the red.

As these patterns became common throughout publishing, an increasing number of editors, who were feeling the pressure to produce higher profits, left the firm after only a short tenure. Agents increasingly became the fixed point in authors' lives, the only people who they could feel sure would be there to work with them in the future. But from these reasonable and understandable circumstances, a new system developed that was to have disastrous consequences in the long run.

When I started out in publishing, the option clause in a contract had real meaning. The author promised to offer his or her next book to an editor, and, in most cases, the editor would feel bound to take it on. Publishers were known for issuing the collected works of major authors, and it was a matter of pride at Knopf, for instance, that the dozens of books written by the most famous Japanese authors were all linked to Harold Strauss, Knopf's very knowledgeable editor in that field. It was also unusual for an established author to be told that a new book was not likely to sell enough copies to justify Knopf's publishing it. When Alfred Knopf was sent *The Black Swan* by Thomas Mann, he did not respond by saying that he preferred to wait until something a little more commercial came along.

As agents became more important, these considerations fell by the wayside. A book would no longer be sent only to the author's former publisher but to half a dozen other potential customers. An auction would replace the former negotiations in which the publisher had the right to make an acceptable offer as part of the option clause. As Michael Korda recalls in his memoir, some agents would offer books by celebrity authors without informing the writer they were putatively representing. If anyone took the bait, the agent would then approach the author with an enticing offer.

The situation was already fraught when negotiations were carried out for sums that everyone involved agreed on. But increasingly reason was abandoned as well, by both publishers and agents. Faced with a need to maintain their hold on leading authors or else find others that would guarantee them best-sellers, publishers became willing to make less money on their leading titles or even to turn them into loss leaders. Agents were quick to see this change and played it for all it was worth.

Unwilling to participate in this game, the editors at Pantheon sought other ways to find books that might sell in large numbers. We were concerned that younger people, even university students, were becoming reluctant to read the traditional classics. We spent a great deal of time looking for formats that were more accessible and visually appealing. Help in these endeavors came, unexpectedly, from the Third World. A Mexican political cartoonist and commentator known as Rius had published a heavily illustrated paperback called *Marx for Beginners*. Though not quite a comic book, it used pictures very effectively and conveyed the essence of Marx's thought in an easily comprehensible way. The book had sold tremendously well in Mexico and had been translated into English by Writers and Readers, a small left-wing cooperative in London run by an energetic group of young editors. I offered a substantial advance on future books allowing Writers and Readers to develop a series. A large number of titles followed, distilling the works of thinkers such as Albert Einstein and Sigmund Freud. I approached my old Cambridge friend Jonathan Miller and suggested he contribute a volume on Charles Darwin, which went on to achieve great success. By the time our collaboration ended, the Beginner's books had sold over a million copies and were widely used in high schools and universities throughout the country. We also published a number of avant-garde graphic novels, the most successful of which was Art Spiegelman's book about the Holocaust, *Maus*. Turned down by dozens of American publishers, it sold in the hundreds of thousands in the United States and went on to win the Pulitzer Prize.

Although I was trying to find books that appealed to readers who were more attracted by images than words, I was nevertheless reluctant to sign up books of photography, about which I knew little. But through the American historian Warren Sussman we received an extraordinary doctoral thesis that attempted to present the psychohistory of a small town in Wisconsin around the turn of the nineteenth century by using the archives of a local photographer. *Wisconsin Death Trip* by Michael Lesy used a wide range of glass negatives, from traditional marriage portraits to photographs commemorating the not-infrequent deaths of babies. So startling were these images that some stores initially refused to stock the book. Lesy had managed the rare task in post-1960s America of finding visual images that could shock and astonish, just as Luis Buñuel had done in his early films. The book became an extraordinary commercial success, and we went on to publish a series of Lesy's quirky and provocative archives of the American past.

The unexpected success of Lesy's book emboldened me to look further into photography. Susan Meiselas's stunning book of color photographs of Nicaragua significantly affected contemporary perceptions of Central America. We also published *Secret Paris of the Thirties* by the renowned French photographer Brassaï in an edition that proved to be more popular than its French equivalent. Brassaï's work led us to other similar discoveries from the past, including Walker Evans's fascinating documentation of Havana in the 1940s, Robert Frank's later work, and the first complete collection of Laszlo Moholy-Nagy's Bauhaus photographs. As we became known for our success with books on photography, we were able to publish more commercially successful photographers such as Annie Leibovitz and Helmut Newton in books that helped to meet the ever-growing pressure for higher sales from the management of Random House.

For a while, I thought we might be able to break out of the trap set by Newhouse's profit expectations by expanding Pantheon through acquisitions. If Pantheon could find a suitable firm to buy, we could add to the annual turnover and increase our backlist sales, as others had done. Newhouse favored such purchases and even proposed some possible candidates to us. But the lists suggested did not seem strong enough or of sufficient interest. If we could find the right firm, however, and could integrate it successfully, Pantheon might make more money. I was therefore very interested when, in 1987, I was approached by lawyers asking if we would take on Schocken Books.

Over the years, practically since the beginning of my time with Pantheon, I had worked with the people running Schocken. I felt a strong sense of kinship with this exile publisher who had fled Germany as a result of the war, setting up shop first in Jerusalem and then, in 1945, in the United States. Schocken represented an impressive German-Jewish tradition. Though I was not personally close to the religious positions of the house, I had read and admired many of their authors, including Martin Buber, Gershom Scholem, and Walter Benjamin. In the past, Hannah Arendt had briefly worked for Schocken as an editor; the descendants of the Schocken family maintained the high intellectual standards that had marked the firm since its inception.

During the curious phase in the 1930s when the Nazis encouraged separate Jewish cultural activity in order to segregate it more clearly from the rest of German culture, Joseph Goebbels decreed that Schocken become the publisher of Franz Kafka and other German-Jewish writers. Kafka thus moved from Kurt Wolff's publishing house, where he had been launched, and became an essential part of the Schocken backlist. Goebbels could not have foreseen that this action would, in time, be crucial in sustaining Schocken's role as a leading Jewish publisher.

Schocken had never been very profitable and had been maintained by the family's holdings in real estate, just as the original Schocken had been subsidized by a department store in Berlin. The purchase price, by Newhouse standards, was small, and I felt it was important to provide a safe haven for the company. I insisted to Newhouse's people that such a deal would make sense and, after months of detailed investigation, an agreement was made. It later struck me as ironic that a purchase that entailed so little risk should have been made with such care, while the far more dubious purchase of Crown was made so peremptorily.

With the financial pressures from Newhouse intensifying, the thought of relaunching Schocken gave me a new lease on life. We decided not merely to reissue the old books, but to deal with them in a manner worthy of their importance. New translations of Kafka's work were commissioned, under the editorship of Mark Anderson of Columbia University's German department. Previously untranslated material from Kafka's oeuvre was included. We took on a series of books, some dealing with Israel and Eastern Europe, and others on the history of World War II. Schocken's excellent list on the Holocaust was brought back into print, though I was shocked to hear from one of Random House's (Jewish) vice presidents, Bruce Harris, that he wished we "would stop hitting him over the head with all these Holocaust titles" because they were not going to make enough money.

By the fall of 1989, our joint list had grown substantially, and I was proud of the books we had added to the imprint. But because we wanted to remain faithful to the company's history and its authors, the possibility of quick profits was ruled out. In the first years our investment lost money, since the repackaging of the list and the retranslation of Kafka were expensive undertakings.

In the end what appeared at first to be a temporary solution to Pantheon's problems with Random House became, in fact, the source of additional pressure on an already strained relationship. Pantheon's future was clearly at risk. Despite continuing protestations of Newhouse's good intentions, rumor had it that he was eager to shut Pantheon down. Only Bernstein's support, it was said, kept the list alive. During the 1980s, Pantheon's program continued to strengthen, with sales growing steadily and a variety of books making the *Times* best-seller list, from Anita Brookner's novels to George Kennan's works of history and politics.

But then Newhouse decided that Bernstein should step down. With the same brutality that had marked the sackings of various editors of Newhouse's magazines, Bernstein's "resignation" was announced to a startled publishing world in 1989. The front page of the *Times* noted the event and devoted several articles to it, few of which drew any of the obvious conclusions about what was in store for Random House. The future became very apparent when Newhouse brought in Alberto Vitale as Bernstein's successor. Vitale had begun his career in Italy as a banker and had moved to New York to become head of the American holdings of the Bertelsmann corporation, then comprising only Doubleday, Bantam, and Dell. It was rumored that Vitale was about to be fired from this post when he was approached by Newhouse with the offer of what was widely considered to be the most important job in American publishing. Newhouse is a shy and diffident man, as is clear from his biographies, but he was clearly attracted to his opposite, the businessman with a thuggish disposition and a thoroughly anti-intellectual attitude—the pose of the rough-and-ready street fighter who gets things done and isn't afraid to do what it takes to make as much money as possible.

Placing a philistine businessman at the head of a publishing house was nothing new. Eugene Exman tells of the new president of Harper's in 1915, C. T. Brainderdin, who was known for saying, "There is no person here who cannot be replaced by a ten-dollar-a-week clerk," and who cut back on advertising and other frills so that in a very short time he had lost Sinclair Lewis to Harcourt, James Branch Cabell to McBride, and Theodore Dreiser to Boni and Liveright. Having thus disposed of most of the firm's literary stars, he was left only with more popular authors like Zane Grey. His competitors were of course delighted and doubtless agreed with his analysis of how replaceable he himself might have been.

Vitale was introduced by Newhouse as a man of culture and sensitivity, a description soon undermined by Vitale's admission that he was far too busy to read a book (although he did eventually agree to read the novels of Judith Krantz, Crown's best-selling romance author). In a skyscraper where nearly every office was lined with books, Vitale's offered a stark contrast. Not a book could be seen on his shelves; the photographs on display were not of authors but of his yacht.

When I first met Vitale at Newhouse's luxurious East Side townhouse, he greeted me with the words "Ah, Pantheon, where all those marvelous books come from." What I took as a compliment was really an accusation. No sooner was Vitale in place than rumors began to swirl anew about Pantheon's imminent demise. It was only later that I realized this was part of the standard Newhouse corporate modus operandi, where rumor was used to attack the position of anyone in disfavor, either by weakening their bargaining position or by preparing them for an eventual sacking. Although Random House was losing huge amounts of money on Crown, attention was soon focused instead on Pantheon's inadequate profitability.

Initially, we thought the rumors were simply that: the kind of speculation that publishing loves to indulge in, the schadenfreude that came with the thought that someone else was about to be pulled down. We had no idea how carefully the rumors had been orchestrated. Indeed, when I went back through my correspondence of the period, I found letters I had written in the middle of January 1990 reassuring friends in England who had heard we might be in trouble. I went so far as to suggest to Vitale that he publicly denounce the rumors, putting to rest the speculation that we were on his hit list. We wrote a press release that we suggested he issue, pointing to the fact that Pantheon was publishing an exceptionally strong list, its best ever, I felt, and that its profitability was about to improve markedly. We had just signed on a series of books by Matt Groening based on a new television series called *The Simpsons*. We had no idea these books would eventually sell millions of copies, but we knew that the list scheduled for 1990 would make as much money as any Pantheon had published, and that if the Groening books performed as we expected, we were likely to be among Random's most profitable holdings.

However, in a series of meetings to which I was summoned, it soon became clear that Pantheon's fate had already been decided. Vitale initially suggested that we might stand to make a good deal more if we were to cut our list and staff by two-thirds and concentrate on the books with the largest printings. In response, I insisted that the corporation's accountants prepare a budget. It showed that Pantheon would be far *less* profitable if it made cuts in the draconian manner proposed.

One crucial meeting in January demonstrated how far apart we were. Vitale looked through the books that we were about to publish for spring 1990, a list we were particularly proud of. "Who is this

Claude Simon?" he asked disdainfully, having clearly never heard of the Nobel Prize-winning novelist, "and this Carlo Ginzburg?" probably Italy's best-known historian. I then noticed that he would begin reading on the right side of the page, where the print runs were listed, and only then moved to the puzzling titles. For him, it was as if we were a shoe manufacturer, making sizes too small to fit most customers. "What is the sense of publishing books with such small printings?" he shouted. Were we not ashamed of ourselves? How could I face myself in the mirror each morning knowing that I wanted to publish such hopelessly unprofitable titles? The list included Groening's books, which, according to our reckoning, would more than amply pay for the losses that might be incurred by the more difficult books. But Vitale's new policy was that each book should make money on its own and that one title should no longer be allowed to subsidize another.

The reduction of the list and staff was only a part of the agenda. Vitale told me very clearly, though he denied it afterward, that we should stop publishing "so many books on the left" and instead publish more on the right. It was clear that Newhouse had been unhappy with the publication of titles whose politics he disliked, and evidently their elimination was one of the reasons Pantheon had risen to the top of the list of problems to be solved. Newhouse, whose politics were known to be markedly rightist ever since college, had objected as much to Bernstein's publication of Soviet dissidents as to ours of American ones. Within a few months, both of these thorns would be removed from his side.

As discussions continued, I began to realize that we were involved in a farcical, purely symbolic exercise. What was going on was more like a plant closing than the discussion of the future of a publishing house. We had assumed that we were dealing with interlocutors who would state their views honestly and listen to ours with some degree of openness. It became clear that this was not the case: promises made by Vitale in one session were vehemently denied by him and his subordinates in the next. This constant shifting persuaded me that our discussions were meaningless. Newhouse and Vitale wanted either to cut Pantheon as a prelude to closing it, or to discourage my colleagues and me so completely that we would leave of our own accord.

When Tom Mayer wrote a long and perceptive piece in *Newsday* about our story, which later appeared in his biography of Newhouse, he described Pantheon as very much an island within the Random House sea. He reported that our Random colleagues found us distant and different — much more so than I realized at the time.

During the 1970s, when Pantheon's interests became clear to the rest of the world, it was not difficult to find able and committed young people who shared our outlook and were willing to come work for us, even though our salaries were far from the highest in the industry. To find the interest and skills we needed, I had looked outside of publishing more than from within. Though we always had one editor from professional publishing who concentrated on the more commercial titles, most of my colleagues came from the academy. Sara Bershtel had been a professor of comparative literature for many years. An able critic, familiar with many of the languages with which we worked, she was responsible for much of what we published from Europe as well as American authors like Barbara Ehrenreich. Jim Peck and Tom Engelhardt came from the

Committee of Concerned Asian Scholars, an ad hoc group that had been created during the Vietnam War, and had been the editors of the Committee's influential *Bulletin*. Both were dedicated scholars. Jim continued to focus in this area, but branched out into working with such authors as Fulbright and Chomsky. Tom, the editor of Art Spiegelman's *Maus*, also moved into other areas, particularly within popular culture. Wendy Wolf, who would later play a crucial role as the editor of the Groening books, had started at a young age in Pantheon's juvenile department. After a brief stay there, she learned her trade in a long apprenticeship with us, becoming a highly skilled editor. The last of the group, Susan Rabiner, joined us much later, coming from Oxford University Press. A highly professional and energetic editor, she took on much of the makeover of Schocken Books.

Gradually we built up a group of intelligent and able people, each with very clear areas of expertise, each able to develop his or her own lists of authors. Uniquely, we worked together as a group with very few of the rivalries that one expects to find in any corporation. The importance of the ideas with which we were working outweighed other considerations and a cohesive group was formed that held together to the very end.

I knew my colleagues had no intention of going along with the dismantling of Pantheon. When it became apparent that some of them might be sacked, they made it clear to me that they would resign en masse. I urged the younger people, including Susan, who had only recently joined us, to wait until they found appropriate jobs elsewhere, but I could see their minds were set. Consequently, I told Vitale and his colleagues that his plan would not work and that I, too, would have to leave since Pantheon as a group effort would no longer exist. The warnings were discounted. People do not normally give up a comfortable position in publishing with nowhere else to go. Instead, they stay behind to argue that they, rather than their colleagues, should stay on, hoping to carry on profitably under new circumstances. The prospect that my colleagues, as a group, might act on principle must have seemed incredible to the Random House bosses.

Certainly from the accounts we received later, it seems that the mass resignation of the Pantheon staff caused great surprise. My colleagues, many of whom had come of age in the 1960s, were familiar with techniques for organizing protests and within a few days, letters were flying to our authors and others throughout the world, seeking their support and urging protest. Unprecedented media interest was aroused. Several hundred people, including authors such as Kurt Vonnegut and E. P. Thompson, as well as a sizable group of people from New York publishing, demonstrated in front of the Random House building. Studs Terkel was literally on the barricade. Moreover, he turned away offers of gigantic advances and kept his next manuscript waiting until we could publish it at The New Press, which had not yet been formed. Hundreds of protest letters were sent to Vitale and a full-page advertisement appeared in the *New York Review of Books*, signed by every manner of author, including many published by Random House. An editorial appeared in the trade journal *Publishers Weekly*, lamenting Vitale's and Newhouse's decisions and asking that they be reversed. The critic John Leonard broadcast an eloquent defense of what Pantheon had stood for on CBS's *Sunday Morning*.

All this was in stark contrast to the lack of support coming from our colleagues within Random House and Knopf. We felt strongly that our stand was in defense of all the editors in Newhouse's companies. We were certain the pressures we were objecting to would not be limited to Pantheon. As Vitale admitted in a later interview, he had to make an example of Pantheon since we had been the most adamant in insisting that our profits from commercially successful books should be used to underwrite the costs of more demanding titles. Knopf and Random had published a substantial number of these less lucrative books over the years, and if Pantheon was to be barred from this sort of publishing, it was likely that they would be, too.

To our surprise, far from believing that we were acting with their interests in mind, nearly all of the editors at the other houses took a strong line of support for Vitale's position. Instigated by two senior editors, a statement was circulated stating that our position was totally unreasonable, that there was no conflict between meeting the company's profit goals and the publication of worthwhile books. A handful of courageous editors, such as Vicky Wilson and Bobbie Bristol at Knopf, refused to sign this loyalty oath and were given a rough time in the months that followed. But forty or so Random House and Knopf editors did sign, including many we considered old friends. None of them called me to find out what was really going on, not a single one asked for details about the discussions between ourselves and Vitale. I assumed they had been told not to talk to us.

Some went further. Those editors who had ties to European publishers made a series of phone calls trying to discourage the impressive protests overseas that had taken place on our behalf. Others were active in trying to prevent the possibility that attractive job offers might be made to me. A search committee for Harvard University Press had asked if I would speak to them about succeeding Arthur Rosenthal, their highly accomplished director who was retiring at the time. Arthur strongly urged me to apply and though I had reservations about moving to Cambridge, I decided I would meet with the committee. Later we discovered that there were two senior Knopf editors who had both put in a number of calls to their friends and authors at Harvard, urging them to dissuade the Press from offering me the job. Presumably my moving to Harvard would have been seen as validation of the role I had played at Pantheon, and it was felt important to prevent this from happening.

It was striking that Random House's efforts, both in their publicity campaign and in private discussions, were focused so heavily on making sure that Pantheon was completely discredited. We were cast as entirely unrealistic people whom no one would wish to hire. The line given to the *New York Times* and other papers was that publishing is too serious a business to be left to intellectuals. Even proven businessmen like Bernstein, it was argued, had shown they were not tough enough to meet the needs of the modern corporation, allowing all sorts of books that did not make money to be published. Pantheon was an extreme case where the editors were not only willing to lose money but actually believed in doing so.

The major papers generally went along with this rationale, though some did come to our defense or at least took a wait-and-see attitude. The response in Europe was the reverse. A raft of articles appeared in defense of Pantheon and what it stood for, speaking out so effectively that Random House was forced to try to intervene, sending fraudulent claims of our losses abroad in the hope of countering the wave of indignation. When persuasion failed to work, Vitale resorted to coercion. I later learned from authoritative sources that Vitale threatened to withhold all future Random House advertising in *Publishers Weekly* if it continued its support of Pantheon.

Just a few years later, this whole process was repeated when Bob Gottlieb was summarily fired from his job as editor-in-chief of the *New Yorker*. Bob had been a close friend and adviser of Newhouse's and thought he had his boss's full confidence. He had very much wanted to be at the *New Yorker*, in spite of the staff uproar that had followed William Shawn's dismissal. Newhouse had promised the people at the *New Yorker* that he would preserve the magazine's integrity, as many still felt deeply betrayed by the way Shawn had been forced out. But Bob was far more faithful to the Shawn heritage than Newhouse had expected, and it was not long before he, too, was given his marching orders. Rumors of his imminent firing had been circulating for some time in New York when Bob was awakened in the middle of the night in Tokyo, where he was visiting, with the news that the articles appearing that day in the *New York Times* about his publishing demise were not exaggerated. Newhouse's propaganda machine then began its spin, insisting that the Shawn-Gottlieb years, clearly the most important in the magazine's history, were an unfortunate deviation from the publication's original lighthearted mission. When the *New York Times* polled various magazine editors on the change, only Rick MacArthur, the courageous publisher of *Harper's*, was willing to challenge the Newhouse line. Otherwise, Gottlieb was consigned to the dustbin of history as effectively as if he had been an offending page in the Great Soviet Encyclopedia, to be torn out, denied, and forgotten.

It was clear that at the time of our so-called negotiations Vitale and his Random House colleagues followed a pre-established scenario, one that had been used many times before. Just as Random's personnel department had a box of tissues at the ready and a brief on how to prepare a résumé for people who were fired, so Vitale prepared his "negotiations." The first step was to deny me the right to have someone of my choosing with me when I made my case. I had wanted one of my editors to accompany me so that they would be fully informed as to what was happening. The point was to keep me from having any witnesses when promises that had been made were later denied.

The other weapon, which was used as effectively, was a clause in my agreement to leave that stated that neither party could speak to the press for the next five years about the internal discussions that had taken place at Random House then or before. While Newhouse had a reputation for buying people off with very generous golden handshakes, the negotiations that led to my departure were extremely hard-nosed. It was clear that the best I could hope for was the amount of money that I had been guaranteed in my contract; "Not a nickel more," the Random House treasurer later advised me. This money was not severance pay; it was due to me contractually —I had earned it over the years in Random House's equivalent of a pension fund. Random withheld the money for six months after I signed the agreement, in effect forcing me to keep silent while the company issued various statements attacking Pantheon and myself. The *New York Times* duly reported that I was "unavailable for comment" but only one journalist sought comment from any of my colleagues, who could have told them what had happened equally well. The Pantheon editors who left with me had courageously done so without any severance agreements and therefore were free to answer any questions. So, too, could Bob Bernstein or Tony Schulte, both of whom had been fully aware of Pantheon's finances over the years. The fact that our profitability had never troubled the previous Random House regime was not something that the press looked into. The argument was carried on in a very simple, one-sided fashion, fueled by the Random House spin doctors, who poured out phony arguments and falsified figures.

Within days Vitale hired Fred Jordan to run the list, though he was to stay for only the briefest of periods. Jordan was an editor whose European background contributed to the illusion that he would continue to pursue the tradition that Pantheon had built. However, true to the intentions of his employers, Jordan met with the few people remaining in the Pantheon offices and announced in his opening statement that Pantheon would no longer publish political works. In the years to follow, the imprint abandoned every aspect of its previous program and was entirely subsumed under Knopf's control. Jordan lasted barely beyond his first year in the Pantheon offices. The books that had raised questions about broader social issues vanished, as did the more demanding intellectual and cultural titles. One of the lead titles published under the Pantheon imprint in the fall of 1998 was a collection of photographs of Barbie dolls. As for Schocken, Random House kept the name alive but shifted its emphasis to a few commercial titles every year — books on Jewish cooking, family life, and spirituality.

Ironically, many of those who had signed the statement denouncing us soon departed, for reasons very similar to those that had forced the de facto closure of Pantheon. The case of Times Books is illuminating in this regard. As its name suggests, the imprint was originally linked to the *New York Times* and devoted to publishing its reporters. As time passed, more famous and sellable names, such as Boris Yeltsin and Nancy Reagan, were added to the list. But the focus still remained on politics and current affairs. In 1997, Vitale decided this approach was insufficiently profitable and both of its directors, Peter Osnos and Steve Wasserman, left in response to the changes that were imposed. They told me of their conversations with Vitale, in which approaches subtler than those employed at Pantheon were taken to try to make their firm more commercial, but with the same ultimate results. They were such able editors, they were assured, that it seemed a shame for them to waste their talents on books, no matter how worthy, which had only limited sales. Times Books had just published Theodore Draper's massive study of the American constitution, a book that had received widespread praise. However, according to Vitale, it had not sold well enough and it would be better if Osnos and Wasserman spent more time on books like the collected speeches of Bill Clinton. This was indeed among the last books that Times published, advancing in huge numbers, and coming back from the stores in record numbers as well.

Even the highly profitable Knopf list gradually jettisoned the more demanding translations and works of philosophy and art criticism on which it had built its reputation. Random House itself became more downmarket, competing with Knopf for titles it was hoped would bring in the millions that were essential to the machine. The system of allowing competing entities from within the firm to bid against each other, indeed urging them to do so, raised advances and ratcheted up commitments to advertising and publicity.

The reason I've gone into such detail here is not because I feel that what happened at Pantheon was in any way unique. On the contrary, the more I talk to colleagues, the more I realize that what we experienced is standard procedure in many publishing houses. Millions of workers involved in plant closings have experienced something infinitely harder. Their dismissals rarely warrant press attention. The amount of money they receive from their severance or pension payments is seldom enough to pay for their survival over the following months. It is obvious, if rarely discussed, that many of the most important aspects of society are governed not by public entities but by private ones. Corporations entirely control who works and how they work. Employees have no right to protest or, in many cases, even negotiate. There is no question of due process and, as my lawyers have told me, there are very few effective grounds for legal action.

In our case, it was evident that the company's intention was not simply to get rid of those who dissented but to make it clear that there were no alternatives. The corporation and its program were above all criticism and those who begged to differ were irresponsible troublemakers to be pilloried in the press and drummed out of the profession. No matter that the new plans proved unenforceable and the losses incurred by Random ballooned beyond anything that had come before. What mattered was power. The company, like the party or the government, had to be right. Everything might come crashing down at a later date, but, for the time being, there could be no questions. The one possible check on this kind of arbitrary action is criticism from the press and the public. But corporate affairs of this sort, in publishing or anywhere else, are rarely discussed openly.

FOUR

Market Censorship

THE RECENT changes in publishing discussed in these pages demonstrate the application of market theory to the dissemination of culture. After the pattern of Ronald Reagan's and Margaret Thatcher's probusiness policies, the owners of publishing houses have increasingly "rationalized their activities." The market, it is argued, is a sort of ideal democracy. It is not up to the elite to impose their values on readers, publishers claim, it is up to the public to choose what it wants—and if what it wants is increasingly downmarket and limited in scope, so be it. The higher profits are proof that the market is working as it should.

Traditionally, ideas were exempted from the usual expectations of profit. It was often assumed that books propounding new approaches and different theories would lose money, certainly at the outset. The phrase "the free marketplace of ideas" does not refer to the market value of each idea. On the contrary, what it means is that ideas of all sorts should have a chance to be put to the public, to be expressed and argued fully and not in soundbites.

For much of the twentieth century, trade publishing as a whole was seen as a break-even operation. Profit would come when books reached a broader audience through book clubs or paperback sales. If this was true of nonfiction, it was doubly true of literature. Most first novels were expected to lose money (and many authors have been described as writing a lot of first novels). Nonetheless, there have always been publishers who regard publishing new novelists as an important part of their overall output.

New ideas and new authors take time to catch on. It might be years before a writer finds an audience large enough to justify the costs of publishing her book. Even in the long run the market cannot be an appropriate judge of an idea's value, as is obvious from the hundreds, indeed thousands, of great books that have never made money. Thus, the new approach—deciding to publish only those books that can be counted on for an immediate profit—automatically eliminates a vast number of important works from catalogs.

There is a further complication. While fiction and poetry may well be written by authors working full-time elsewhere, authors of important works of nonfiction require advances or some other form of assistance to enable them to undertake their research. It is in this area of important work that we have seen the sharpest decline. The "mute, inglorious Milton" of Gray's *Elegy Written in a Country Churchyard* has been replaced by the "mute, inglorious Foucault," the thinker who does not have the wherewithal to write the book that will change the way we think, which may happen even if only a small number of people buy it.

Finally, as in every other aspect of the free market, there is the problem that the playing field is far from level. The larger firms, publishing the more commercial books, have vast advertising budgets at their disposal, enormous sales forces, and an extremely efficient network of press contacts, all of which helps ensure that their books get a certain amount of attention. Smaller publishers are unable to compete on an equal footing and have a much harder time finding space for their books, both in stores and in review columns.

The prevalence of market ideology has affected other spheres in society that in turn have changed the nature of book publishing. In both the United States and Britain, for example, public library purchases were once large enough to cover most of the costs of publishing meaningful works of fiction and nonfiction. I remember Gollancz would always order the same number of copies of a book from Pantheon — 1,800 — whether it was a mystery or a political treatise. Intrigued, I eventually asked him why this number. Simple, he answered. He could count on orders for 1,600 copies from Britain's libraries. When, in recent years, library funding was drastically cut, an infrastructure supporting the publication of many challenging books was leveled.

But this is only one of many forces affecting the demise of "challenging" books. The change in editorial procedures at large firms has also had a broad impact. This process has been skewed by the fact that decisions on what to publish are made not by editors but by so-called publishing boards, where the financial and marketing staff play a pivotal role. If a book does not look as if it will sell a certain number — and that number increases every year (it's about 20,000 in many of the larger houses today) — then the publishing board decides that the company cannot afford to take it on. This is usually the case when a new novel or a work of serious nonfiction is being discussed. What *El País* called "market censorship" is increasingly in force in the decision-making process based on the requirement of a pre-existing audience for any book.[24]

In the past, an editor would be asked to estimate the sales of the titles he or she proposed. But of course these calculations, infused by the editor's commitment to the book's ideas, were often unreliable, so print runs gradually became the province of sales people. Nowadays, the figure settled upon is usually decided according to what the author's previous book has sold. This has necessarily led to a marked conservatism, both aesthetic and political, in what is chosen: a new idea, by definition, has no track record.

For obvious reasons, editors have been reluctant to talk about the commercial pressures they face. A rare exception, reported by Janice Radway in *A Feeling for Books*, is Marty Asher, now head of Vintage but at the time with the Book-of-the-Month Club. In an interview with him in 1990, Asher said,

> When you get a large corporation taking over they're interested in the bottom line.... Some of them are just merciless, you know "if it doesn't make money we don't want it." Of course if you applied that logic you'd probably eliminate half of the most successful books ever published because it takes a while and nobody wants to wait.... The house I came from, if you couldn't get out 50,000 copies they didn't want to bother. It just wasn't worth it. In a mass market now you're talking 100,000 copies.

In time, the system became even more "scientific." Just as an editor was required to run a "profit-and-loss statement" on each book before being allowed to sign it up, a similar running "P & L" is now kept on the editor themselves, with each editor expected to bring in a certain amount of money every year. Strict controls are maintained on editorial choices. The big companies impose sales quotas, so that even Oxford University Press demands that a young editor sign up enough books in a year to bring in a million dollars —obviously discouraging the acquisition of smaller, more challenging titles. Young editors often tell me exactly what the return on their investments have been down to the last decimal point. These numbers determine their salary and status. It is now extremely difficult to publish smaller books: editors see that their own careers will be hampered if they are identified with such titles. The more an editor spends, the more promising he or she seems. Young people in particular have realized that the way to make their mark is to give authors as large an advance as possible, as early in their own careers as they can. Many will have moved on to other firms by the time the book is published and has failed to earn out its advance.

Caught up in this financial machinery, editors are perceptibly— and understandably—less willing to take a gamble on a challenging book or a new author. And the system has become internalized. Publishers and editors alike now explain that they "can no longer afford" to take on a certain kind of book. Literary agents complain bitterly about these changes. The fall 1999 issue of the newsletter of the Association of Authors' Representatives quotes one of its members as saying, "These mergers have increased the obsession with the bottom line. I can't tell you how many editors say to me these days, 'We aren't buying mid-list.' They want everything totally assured up front." Even houses as successful as Knopf now reject books in areas in which they had traditionally published, explaining that they "can no longer afford to do these books," though the profits generated by Knopf are a major source of income for the Random House group. I used to joke with my editors that we were being paid in kind, that a good part of our salary consisted of the books that we could do when we wanted to do them. This kind of thinking is now safely eliminated from the major publishing houses in the United States and increasingly in Europe as well. A look at some of the major American houses clearly reveals this transformation.

The paperback industry has not been exempt from these pressures. When I was studying in England, a Penguin book would sell for around 2 shillings and 6 pence, or 35 cents. This was in keeping with the prices being charged in the United States for equivalent paperbacks and clearly did not bring in enormous profits. After Pearson's takeover, the existing backlist titles, whether fiction or nonfiction, were reprinted in a larger trade paperback format and prices increased dramatically. The original trade paperback in America, a format started in the 1950s, had been only a little more expensive than the mass-market paperbacks with which I was working. The first list of trade paperbacks issued by Anchor Books ranged in price from 65 cents to $1.25. For many years the average Vintage book, still in its smaller format, was $1.95. Marginally increasing the size of the books, Vintage ultimately increased its prices to $10 and above. I remember at the time arguing that this would greatly diminish the number of people buying new Vintage books. "You may be right," I was told, "but the dollars will remain the same." This phrase seems to me to mark the transition from the old ideology to the new. The idea that a book ought to be inexpensive in order to reach as broad a public as possible was being replaced by accounting decisions that looked only at cash totals. It was not a question of simply making money or avoiding a loss — the Vintage list, consisting of the best backlist titles from Random House, Knopf, and Pantheon, was already guaranteed a substantial annual profit. The rule now was that profit *per book sold* had to be as high as possible.

The changes that took place in the United States have been replicated in Britain. The smaller British houses have disappeared into the hands of the conglomerates controlled by Murdoch, Pearson, and Random House. Newhouse showed his usual recklessness when he bought into the British publishing scene. A distinguished trio of old independent houses — Jonathan Cape, Chatto & Windus, and The Bodley Head — had banded together to share distribution and other costs, but had nevertheless fallen upon hard times. It was widely known in London publishing circles that the firms were for sale and could be had for a song. One publisher told me that he had refused an offer to take the houses in exchange for covering their debts. Newhouse, however, seeing a prestigious entry into the British market, offered over £10 million to the startled owners, who took the money and ran. Thus was born the Newhouse colony in Britain. Other once-famous firms, including Heinemann and Secker & Warburg, were subsequently added to the fold.

As a result of these amalgamations London soon had as few independent houses as New York. It is estimated that in the 1950s London had about two hundred significant publishers. Now there are less than thirty. In the last months, some of the few remaining holdouts, including the Hodder-Headline group, have been bought out — in this case by the magazine and newspaper distributors W. H. Smith, leaving behind a mere handful of independents such as Faber & Faber, Granta, and Fourth Estate, as well as a small number of tiny new houses, which, following the American model, have been created by editors fleeing the wreckage of the large groups.

Meanwhile Penguin, under Pearson's ownership, has proceeded to buy up a large number of once-independent hardcover houses, acquiring Michael Joseph, Hamish Hamilton, Ladybird, and the publisher of the Beatrix Potter children's books. Penguin, however, must be given credit for having found structural ways of maintaining its production of serious nonfiction. In its most recent reconfiguration, the company was divided into two halves, one commercial, the other, renamed the Penguin Press, devoted to serious work in the humanities and sciences. Each half of the firm was allocated a share of the profits from the enormous Penguin backlist so that the Penguin Press could use the income from Penguin Classics to help pay for books such as a multivolume biography of Lloyd George. Had Pantheon been able to draw on Vintage profits in a similar way, its earnings would have been assured in perpetuity. The Penguin experiment is unique in British publishing and shows that a management determined to maintain high standards can do so, if it chooses.

But overall, during the Thatcher years, British media was transformed for the worse. Thatcher's emphasis on money and market values was echoed in book publishing itself. New bosses who were brought into the larger groups such as Reed Elsevier and HarperCollins quickly and forcibly expressed their disdain for the genteel values of their predecessors. Like Vitale at Random, they

wanted to establish early on that they did not care for the old intellectual and cultural standards. They were there to make money and
for no other reason. The yield of the sizable firms changed accordingly. While a few stubborn editors held out, most of my former
associates fell by the wayside. On my yearly visits to London, I
began to feel I was taking part in a geriatric version of Agatha
Christie's *And Then There Were None*. Everyone near my age had
disappeared, either having been fired or bought off into early retire-
ment. Soon it was very hard to find anyone in the business over fifty.
This change resulted largely from narrow financial considerations:
younger people would work for less money than their older predecessors. But the effect was an erasure of corporate memory: those
who remembered the way things used to be done were eliminated
and replaced with a group who automatically saw the new dictates
as normal and indeed right.

All of this has affected not just editors and readers, but others in
the book world as well, particularly salespeople. The semi-annual
sales conferences of American publishers, which in the 1960s were
something like prolonged college parties, are now increasingly tense
and unpleasant. In my last years at Pantheon, I saw how sales reps
I had known for years were drinking heavily during the meetings.
When I talked to them I recognized the pressure they were under
and the ways they were being forced to change their relationship
with booksellers.

Their job used to be representing the bookstores to us as much
as conveying our views of the books to the stores. The system had
a curiously federal touch to it. The reps were wary of piling too
many books into stores and did not want to force-feed the accounts.

But as pressure mounted on editors and publishers to come up with ever larger advances, printings have risen concomitantly. Printed books cannot be allowed to sit in a warehouse—they have to be pushed into stores. The booksellers found themselves loaded down with great quantities of would-be best-sellers, books that failed to meet their potential and were returned with ever-increasing speed. Calvin Trillin once described the shelf life of a book as somewhere between that of milk and yogurt, and we joked that an expiration date ought to be stamped on every book cover. Now the stores do that for us, returning the books faster and faster.

+~+

NEWHOUSE'S DECISION to sell the Random House group in 1998 to the massive German firm Bertelsmann shocked the publishing world. Random was still the leading U.S. publisher even if its reputation had become tarnished. William Styron, one of Random's most important literary authors, was quoted in *The Washington Post* as saying that Random had become so gigantic and bloated that it now no longer mattered to whom it belonged. But in spite of such observations, Random's end came like a thunderbolt out of the murky skies of American publishing. After eight years of Vitale's stewardship, Newhouse decided that the firm would never reach the profitability he had been promised.

There had been no indication that Newhouse was tired of his role as publisher, no hint that Random House was losing money. The figures that came out were surprising even to those who had followed Random House's fortunes closely. In 1997, it was revealed that the company wrote off $80 million of unearnable advances. That is to say, the policy of risking more and more money on books had been an enormous failure. Apart from the write-offs, the house itself had declared a profit of only 0.1 percent, a figure so low that many initially thought the *New York Times* had made a typographical error reporting it. Such profits were far lower than anything Random House had ever recorded in the years before Newhouse took over. Vitale's promises of spectacular increases in profit had clearly been unrealizable. And though Newhouse himself had expressed great interest in his publishing conglomerate, one of his friends was quoted in the *New York Observer* as saying, "He didn't get to be worth billions of dollars by indulging his own intellectual interests." Random House's losses were clearly too much to take.

The sale price was surprising, too. While the value of Random House had risen from the $60 million that Newhouse had paid for it to $800 million or so in the final decade of Bob Bernstein's direction, its growth had slowed markedly during the Vitale years. Random House was sold for a little over a billion dollars, suggesting that in the preceding eight years of profit-obsessed management, the value of the firm had only crept up. Newhouse and Vitale had achieved the remarkable result of lowering the intellectual value of the firm, cheapening its reputation, and losing money, all at the same time.

Similar developments had occurred at the *New Yorker*. Tina Brown left as editor after many years of attempting to raise its circulation. The magazine had usually made money, but Newhouse sought to double its circulation, hoping to increase profits further—

and instead sent it into the red. It is a relatively simple matter to increase magazine circulation by charging very little to new subscribers and buying massive advertising. *New Yorker* spots appeared on television for the first time, but the cost of increasing circulation to close to a million was enormous. Independent estimates of Newhouse's loss in the first decade after he took over came to $175 million, even greater than those at Random House.[25]

Around the same time, Murdoch's HarperCollins announced that it had written off $270 million worth of unearned advances. Apparently unheeded internal memos at Harper's urged a return to the more traditional approach to publishing, suggesting that efforts be focused on trying to rebuild the backlist and that wild speculation on possible best-sellers cease. As part of the attempt to increase profits, HarperCollins decided to discontinue and then sell off its distinguished Basic Books imprint, known primarily for its titles on psychoanalysis and the social sciences. As was the case with Pantheon, Basic had never lost money, but the scale of its publishing was geared to a professional rather than a mass-market readership. Consequently, the books could never sell in large enough quantities to meet Harper's expectations of profit and contribution to overhead. After two years, in which the firm's editors desperately tried to find more popular books, the ax finally fell.

A similar decision was made by Simon & Schuster, which had taken over The Free Press, the most devotedly reactionary of American publishers. During the Reagan years, The Free Press had made a fortune publishing books that were fully in keeping with the political zeitgeist. Subsequently, however, the company lost substantial amounts of money on gambles. A biography of

Hillary Clinton proved to be insufficiently hostile for its intended conservative audience. Determined that such a mistake not be made again, Simon & Schuster gutted The Free Press, keeping its name but turning it primarily into a publisher of business books. Even the revolutionaries of the right discovered that revolutions will devour their children, whatever their political coloration. With these changes, the major conglomerates had all divested themselves of their more intellectual, Pantheon-like divisions.

One might think that such massive losses by the two leaders in corporate makeovers would have given others pause for thought. But as soon as Bertelsmann had taken over Random House, they issued a press release saying they expected Random House to make a 15 percent profit in the next few years. That meant a change in profit from $1 million to $150 million (on their annual sales of a billion or so). At the same time, Bertelsmann's corporate handouts made clear that its American holdings, which now included Random, Bantam, Doubleday, and Dell, would also be expected to deliver the 10 percent annual growth that was policy throughout the company; that is, another $100 million. How all this was to be accomplished was not outlined. Perhaps the most telling statistic published about Bertelsmann is that four thousand accountants were reported to be working at its headquarters — many times the number of editors in all its holdings worldwide. The new combined corporation would be responsible for one out of every three trade books published in the United States and would account for 40 percent of Bertelsmann's worldwide sales. Yet in spite of its gigantic size, appeals by authors' groups and others to the attorney general to investigate possible antitrust infringements went unheeded.

A mammoth new conglomerate was now in charge of a very important part of American publishing. To make matters worse, Bertelsmann proceeded to acquire part of Barnes & Noble's online book-selling operation.

The metamorphosis of publishing is not abating. The French conglomerates regularly announce further purchases abroad, particularly in France and Britain. Hachette recently bought the British Orion group, itself the owners of such distinguished older firms as Weidenfeld and Gollancz. Orion is now reported to be looking for an American firm to buy, perhaps Simon & Schuster. The Anglo-Dutch Reed Elsevier group, which owns *Publishers Weekly*, bought up several of Britain's most distinguished publishing houses including Methuen, Heinemann, and Secker & Warburg, and then resold them to Random House in August 1995, citing inadequate profitability (which was later reported to be 12 percent of sales). A parallel development took place in Sweden when another Dutch firm, Wolter Kluwer, bought Norstedts, the second most important publishing house in the country with an illustrious record stretching back nearly two hundred years. Norstedts's profits were soon deemed insufficient and Kluwer decided to keep only the parts of the company producing legal and reference texts. The general publishing division, whose books had formed a central part of Swedish culture, was cast adrift in search of a potential buyer. It was finally bought by the country's cooperative movement, which, in Sweden, still wields considerable power in retailing and distribution; they integrated it into their publishing holdings. But a great deal of damage had already been done by these changes, and Norstedts lost many of its key authors and much of its momentum.

Reed's and Kluwer's decision to concentrate on reference books and information retrieval represents a general trend. Publishers are talking more and more about concentrating on the profitable tip of the information pyramid. They want to make information that used to be found only in books available through new media. Whatever the merits of this technology, and it is undoubtedly of great importance, there is some concern in the United States that public libraries and other open institutions will have less free access to information as a result of it.

All these mergers invariably follow the same pattern. The conglomerate issues a glowing statement lauding the value of the firm it has bought and promising to maintain its traditions. Everyone is assured that no major changes will be made and that as few people as possible will be fired. Later it is announced that simple economies are essential for the sake of efficiency and that "back office" functions will be merged. Accounting, shipping, and warehousing soon find themselves under a common roof. Then the sales forces are amalgamated, since there is no need to have different people covering the same territory. After that an unfortunate overlap in editorial output is discovered, and rationalizations are seen to be required there, too. A number of editors and their assistants are fired, since, after all, the total number of books being published must decrease. Gradually it becomes difficult to tell which firm is publishing which books. In Random House UK, for instance, the same people are responsible for several lists that were once issued by individual, distinctive, and independent publishing houses; now these companies are merely names to be affixed to the title pages of new books. Older books, meanwhile, are ruthlessly pulped or put out of print if they do not sell an ever stricter minimum amount of copies, often as few as 2,000 a year. As a result, many classics are no longer available. Finally, new imprints are set up to run groups of lists, paperback reprints of older books, and new categories of publishing that can overcome the former, "inefficient" divisions of labor.

As we have seen, accelerating corporatization has been accompanied by an upsurge in the amount of profit sought by the major publishing houses. In American publishing since the 1920s, throughout periods of prosperity and depression, average profit for all of the houses was around 4 percent after taxes. (This includes companies that were intensely commercial, generating only those books they felt to be moneymakers, as well as the more intellectual houses that sought to balance profitability with responsibility.)

It is instructive to look at recent figures for those few houses that have not yet been corporatized. In a fascinating survey of European publishing that appeared in 1996, *Le Monde* provided specific numbers. In France, for instance, the most prestigious of the established book houses, Gallimard, makes an annual profit of a little over 3 percent, despite a strong backlist and a flourishing children's book program. Éditions du Seuil, perhaps the second most impressive of the French independents, comes up with a profit of just over 1 percent. At present, both houses are still owned by the founding families and their allies, but because of internal disputes, Gallimard has had to sell some of its holdings to outsiders and its future independence is not to be taken for granted.

As one publishing house after another has been taken over by conglomerates, the owners insist that their new book arm bring in the kind

of revenue their newspapers, cable television networks, and films do
—businesses that have always enjoyed far higher profit margins. New
targets have therefore been set in the range of 12–15 percent, three to
four times what publishing houses have made in the past.

To meet these new expectations, publishers drastically change
the nature of what they publish. In a recent article, the *New York
Times* focused on the degree to which large film companies are now
putting out books through their publishing subsidiaries, so as to cash
in on movie tie-ins. In 1990, The Disney Corporation established its
own publishing arm, Hyperion, to exploit Disney releases. The thrust
of this effort was described in the *Times* by Robert Gottlieb, a leading agent: "We are not dealing with Farrar, Straus here. Remember
this is a very commercial entertainment business."

Conglomerate publishers are revamping their lines to fit this
description. They are also changing their personnel. Pearson, for
instance, brought in Michael Lynton (since replaced) as the head of
its international book-publishing arm. Soon after his arrival, Lynton,
who had formerly worked for Disney, announced that the famous
Penguin logo would be used to sell related "entertainment products"
such as music. Meanwhile, HarperCollins in New York hired Anthea
Disney as its chief executive (again, only for a short time). She had
previously edited *TV Guide*, one of Murdoch's most lucrative and
popular publications. Last year, a new HarperEntertainment division was established, announcing that in its first years it would publish 136 books, all tie-ins to films and television (such as *The Jerry
Springer Show*), overwhelming the rest of what HarperCollins will
put out. Nevertheless, despite such changes, few houses are able to
reach the new profit targets. Indeed, some of the large corporations

make far less money than they did five years ago when they were pursuing their old diversified policy.

Another effect of corporatization that has rarely been discussed is the issue of growing overhead, which also drives the increasing demand for higher profits. Book publishers have started mimicking the lifestyles of Hollywood moguls. Publishing used to be considered, at least in English-speaking countries, a "profession for gentlemen." That euphemism refers to the payment of comparatively low salaries — book people for many decades were paid at roughly the same levels as academics. Today, publishers have raised their salaries into the millions. A recent *Publishers Weekly* survey showed that the head of McGraw-Hill makes over $2 million a year, more than the CEOs at Exxon or Phillip Morris. In 1998, Viacom's publishing division — part of which was being sold off that year as unprofitable — paid its head $3.25 million. One cannot help but wonder to what degree the lack of profit at Viacom was due to the unrealistic salaries its executives demanded, at the expense of the books and their authors. Other CEOs paid themselves over a million dollars, including some whose firms were performing badly. Richard Snyder, who left Simon & Schuster to buy a publishing house that has yet to show a profit, pays himself some $1.4 million annually.

Overhead has increased in other ways, too. Publishers' offices keep getting more and more expensive, coming to resemble the premises of banks. Random House's sales conferences, often held in deluxe resorts in places like Bermuda and Orange County, were costing a million dollars each by the time I left the company — and these are held twice a year. Editors and publishers have come to expect the comforts of corporate life, expensive restaurants, limousines waiting at their doors, and other status symbols. Rather than taking their reward in books they can be proud of, they look on such luxuries as appropriate recognition. The augmenting overhead that results amounts to a tax, an ever-higher tax, for each publisher. Because these charges are calculated by central accounting, rather than by the individual houses, they are subject to the vagaries of corporate priorities and can therefore be abused, as they were in our final years at Pantheon.

◆

THE CHANGES that have taken place in publishing are increasingly mirrored in the bookselling business as well. One of the first titles I commissioned at Pantheon was a survey of monopoly practices in America. *In a Few Hands* was publicly presented as the work of the late populist senator from Tennessee, Estes Kefauver. In reality, it was written by his very able staff, who ran a series of exemplary hearings over the years on the way monopolies had grown in the American economy. In addition to chapters on the steel industry and pharmaceuticals, the book included an account of a public inquiry into bakeries. C. Wright Mills originally organized the inquiry that showed how national brands such as Tip Top and Wonder had replaced the small bakeries that used to be in every town. The large industrial outfits initially offered bread at prices that greatly undercut local bakeries. They also encouraged local grocery stores to give more shelf space to their bread by hiking up discounts. Price differentials were at first sufficiently attractive to drive the

Twenty Leading Book Cities in 1945
and Number of Independent Bookstores in Each[26]

CITY	STORES
New York	333
Chicago	88
Los Angeles	66
San Francisco	59
Philadelphia	54
Boston	46
Washington, DC	44
Baltimore	32
Seattle	26
Cincinnati	24
Detroit	23
St. Louis	23
Buffalo	20
Dallas	20
Minneapolis	19
Columbus	16
Indianapolis	11
St. Paul	11
Total	915

smaller producers into bankruptcy. Having eliminated the competition, the companies raised their prices in predictable monopolistic succession and Americans were left with plastic-wrapped and plastic-tasting bread that was more expensive than the locally produced loaves it replaced. Only many decades later did specialist bakeries begin to flourish again in large cities, selling excellent but very expensive loaves to the small numbers that can afford them.

The fate of the small American baker has stayed in my mind as I have watched the progressive disappearance of independent bookstores from America's main streets. Such independents should not be romanticized. Many were small, illstocked, and as interested in selling greeting cards and stationery as they were in books. But they were numerous and they were an essential part of American life. A 1945 survey, shown at left, lists the number of stores that were deemed worthy of a visit by a publisher's sales representative. New York had 333 stores, Chicago had 88, and Los Angeles 66. New York now has 76 stores, including many that are part of museums, libraries, and other institutions.

Independent bookstores used to offer an alternative to the uniform product of the mass media. The transformation of American bookselling began well before the chains arrived. Bennett Cerf, in his memoirs, dictated in 1967, described the problems that were already being created by new discount stores. Tellingly, all three of the stores he mentions have since disappeared:

> The discount stores, because they don't carry a complete stock but do carry the best sellers, have hurt the small bookseller. In New York, for example, such a store is right across the street from

Brentano's on Fifth Avenue and right down the street from
Scribner's, and as a result, Scribner's and Brentano's don't sell as
many copies of the top best sellers as they used to, because people
go to Korvette's. . . .[27]

Bennett goes on to describe how difficult it had become to place
more complex books in the independent stores, which were suffering more from the competition with the discounters.

A major source of bookselling in preceding decades was the
large department store. Bennett credits Macy's with having been
the most important outlet for the Modern Library when Random
took it over from Boni and Liveright. But department stores didn't
favor discounting and neither did the thousands of outlets for
paperbacks. Even the book clubs sold their offerings at roughly the
bookstore price.

It was the decision to discount books — particularly best-sellers — that made the chains the phenomenon they are today. In
many cities, the chains were the first to establish major bookstores,
and there is no question that these stores now offer Americans
greater choice than existed before. On the other hand, their progressive expansion has been harmful to the remaining independent
stores. In a statement made to the *Financial Times* at the time of last
year's Frankfurt Book Fair, the German minister of culture (and former publisher) Michael Naumann predicted that if discounting was
allowed in Europe, 80 percent of Germany's four thousand bookstores would fold.

In recent years, the chains have grown dramatically in the
United States and are now selling over 50 percent of all books available for retail. Independent bookstores are down to 17 percent, and

that number is decreasing with every passing year. Price clubs and other discounters play an increasingly important role, as do Internet sellers such as Amazon. These factors have brought about a dramatic decline in the number of independent bookstores, from 5,400 stores in the early 1990s to 3,200 today.

The major chains focus their very considerable resources on best-sellers, to the neglect of other titles, which in turn affects the decisions of publishers. Further, because they control such an important part of the market for books, the chains are now able to demand almost whatever terms they wish from the major publishers, who are pressed to pay large amounts of co-op advertising money if they want their books to be placed prominently in the stores, a service traditional booksellers rendered as a matter of course without charge. Independent bookstores recently won a lawsuit against the major publishers for the way they help the chains. These policies have a negative effect on small publishers who are hard put to pay the extra amount for promotion.

To make matters worse, the chains have aggressively opened new stores close to the most successful independents, sometimes directly across the street (as Bennett observed). As a result, more independents are going out of business every day; in the center of New York only a handful remain — three more have closed in the months I have been working on this book.

Limiting outlets in this way compounds the difficulty faced by smaller publishers. The independent bookstore — which could be counted on to feature a new novel or volume of poems if the staff particularly liked it — is replaced by the large chain store using the most up-to-date marketing techniques. Chains have gone so far as to demand that publishers limit author tours to only their stores. Some authors, such as Stephen King, have refused to go along with such restrictions (King insisted on visiting only independents on his last tour). But important as such gestures are, the monopolistic trend of the larger stores cannot be underestimated.

The managers of chains often come from other fields of retailing, and they have no particular interest in books as such — only in the number of dollars each cubic foot of space can earn. The chains' return practices have also generated a host of problems. I once sat at an American Booksellers Association lunch with the chief buyer of popular fiction for one of the chains, hardly someone on the front lines in defense of high culture. Nevertheless, she was deeply unhappy. Her company guidelines mandated that if a book did not sell a certain number of copies per day during the first week on display, it would be moved to the back of the store and then returned. It did not matter if the reviews were late or the promised appearance on *The Today Show* were delayed. Alfred Knopf's old joke that books were "gone today and here tomorrow" has proved to be the rule as the percentage of books returned has crept steadily upwards from around 20 percent in the 1960s to over 40 percent today.

The same trends have affected book clubs, which, before the advent of chains, were a major purveyor of books to middle America. In its heyday, the Book-of-the-Month Club sold 11 million books a year; close to a million copies per major selection. The Literary Guild was not far behind, and there were dozens of other smaller clubs. (Today the clubs sell far fewer copies and an alternate selection of a major club can ship under 5,000 copies.) The clubs served two overlapping purposes. First, they made books available to a very large audience that had no access to bookstores. Equally important, they chose titles appropriate to their audience rather than simply selecting the book that might sell the largest number of copies. The Book-of-the-Month Club employed an independent panel of judges, including some of the better known critics and authors of the time, to select its titles. While the clubs offered popular fare for the most part, they would occasionally make an unpredictable choice, confirming their independence and distinctive taste.

As time passed, the influence of the judges decreased. The Book-of-the-Month-Club staff would increasingly choose the alternate selections and make crucial marketing decisions. When Time Warner took over the firm the judges were eliminated altogether. *A Feeling for Books*, a fascinating study by the academic anthropologist Janice Radway, includes the reports of a participant observer at the club during the crucial period following the Time Warner takeover. The author describes in touching detail the fears and uncertainties of the staff as they saw their new owners ruthlessly push up the club's profitability and limit their ability to pick books on any other criteria than maximized returns.

In the late 1980s, Bill Zinsser, speaking on the occasion of the Book-of-the-Month-Club's sixtieth anniversary, outlined how the club used to operate:

> If anyone in the room feels strongly that we should take a book, that book will probably be taken, even if it's likely to lose money. Quite often the reasons are public-spirited. It's an important book on an important subject such as nuclear weapons or toxic waste or it's a memoir of a former secretary of state. "We're the book club of

record" someone invariably reminds us and under that commendable rubric, another worthy volume is shepherded into the fold that will bring the club its reward in heaven if not necessarily on the bottom line.

Today, the Book-of-the-Month Club has become nothing more than a mail-order operation. As I was writing the final stages of this book, Bertelsmann announced that merger negotiations had opened between The Literary Guild and the Book-of-the-Month Club. What little competition had existed in the book club business is about to end.

FIVE

Self-Censorship and the Alternatives

I RECENTLY attended a meeting of the Freedom to Read Committee of the Association of American Publishers, the industry's official anticensorship group to which I have belonged on and off over the years. At this particular meeting, a large group of people associated with the anticensorship cause were gathered together. The meeting was held high above Central Park in the extraordinarily luxurious conference room of one of New York's leading law firms, a company that represents the AAP on censorship matters. We sat around a large conference table on a set of chairs that must have cost more than the annual salaries most of us were paying our assistants. The significance of such luxury was not lost on those present.

But the lawyers were speaking to us for our own good. They were concerned that the public's perception of publishers had greatly altered over recent years. They worried that a once worthy

profession had been swallowed up by extensive, wealthy conglomerates. Not surprisingly, when a libel case or other lawsuit
against a publisher was heard, juries were not as sympathetic as
they once had been and the judgments against publishers had
risen accordingly. The lawyers explained that if they could tell
jurors that we were the bastions of the First Amendment, willing
and eager to publish books that expressed important ideas, their
view of us might change perceptibly. Looking at the forty or so of
us who represented most of the major houses in New York, the
lawyers asked, "Can we assure jurors in the future that if an
important book comes along you will publish it?" Not a hand was
raised. No one seemed aware of the irony that the publishing
industry's own anticensorship committee was itself part of the new
market censorship. Evidently surprised, the lawyers continued to
ask questions. Surely, they pleaded, publishers must occasionally
take on a book pro bono, as lawyers sometimes do in representing
impecunious clients. "Only inadvertently," answered the chair of
the group, bringing a wave of relieved laughter and marking an
end to an embarrassing colloquy.

I certainly would not argue that publishers in the past were innocent of attempts at censorship. Going back in history, there is no
lack of egregious examples of editors trying to influence what
authors had to say or refusing their books altogether. Eugene
Saxton, the chief editor of Harper's, declined to publish John Dos
Passos's classic *1919* unless the author removed his criticism of J. P.
Morgan, a major backer of the house. In 1935, when the popular
critic Alexander Wolcott criticized Hitler on a Cream-of-Wheat
sponsored CBS program called *A Town Crier*, the cereal manufac-

turer objected and then canceled the show when Wolcott refused to stop his criticisms. Though Wolcott argued that "anyone with the courage of a diseased mouse" would have done what he did, there is no question that people disseminating ideas are under a lot of pressure from those in power.

Censorship used to come from company bosses who were intolerant toward dissenting opinions. Today, while individual owners are still very concerned with imposing their own views, overall corporate interests have become far more important in controlling the circulation of ideas. The history of Harper's is a good example of this. On the eve of World War II, this company, which had published Leon Trotsky's earlier works, received the blood-splattered galleys of his latest attack on Stalin. The galleys had been on Trotsky's desk when he was murdered by Ramon Sander. Trotsky's followers rushed the galleys to New York on the assumption that they would be published immediately.

The chief editor of Harper's at the time, Cass Canfield, realized that America would soon be at war with Germany and would in time need Stalin's full support. Though he himself was not subjected to any pressure from the government, he called a friend in the state department and discussed the question. Both agreed it would be wiser not to publish the book right away but rather to wait for a more propitious moment. Accordingly, the copies of Trotsky's books that had already been printed were left to gather dust in the Harper's warehouse until the end of the war. Whether Trotsky's critique of Stalin would have influenced American thinking and created a more informed view of Soviet policy during those crucial years is something we will never know. But the decision not to publish and the way it was carried out perfectly symbolized the "responsible," elitist attitude that governed Anglo-American publishing at the time. It seemed the right thing for a citizen to do, even at considerable cost to his firm, and it was carried out without further consultation. One can call this idealistic or patriotic censorship. It was certainly not motivated by a search for profit.

In 1995 Basic Books, the prestigious social science publisher then owned by HarperCollins, published a biography of Deng Xiaoping, written by his daughter.[28] The book itself proved to have no perceptible merit, not even as a document of Chinese hagiography, but Basic launched it with a large publicity campaign reported to have cost at least $100,000 in which the author was brought from China and presented to the press and public. At the time, Murdoch was eager to obtain permission from the Chinese government for his Sky cable network to broadcast in China. He had already agreed to censor the network so that the BBC News, once available to the Chinese, would be blocked. Apparently further persuasion was needed.

To Murdoch, the use of publishing to achieve other ends was simply business as usual. It was exactly the pattern he followed in using his newspapers in Britain and the United States to obtain political favors from different governments. In return for exempting him from British monopoly laws and allowing him to buy several London newspapers, Thatcher was promised their editorial support. In America, as part of a campaign to get licenses for an airline he was starting, Murdoch promised Jimmy Carter, then president, the support of the *New York Post* (traditionally a Democratic party paper anyway). Years later in 1994 a great deal of press coverage was devoted to HarperCollins's decision to pay Newt Gingrich an advance of $4.5 million at the height of the house leader's legislative power (which included important influence over the allocation of television franchises).[29] Less attention was paid to the fact that his book eventually earned a third of that advance, at most.

Another case which aroused considerable interest, this time in Britain, was Murdoch's decision not to publish a book under contract to HarperCollins by the former governor of Hong Kong, Chris Patten. Patten had been a particularly outspoken Conservative opponent of the Chinese government and it was known that his memoirs would be highly critical of it. At the last moment, Murdoch announced that the book would not appear. The book's editor, Stuart Proffitt, the very model of an enlightened Conservative intellectual, resigned and the British press went to town, excoriating Murdoch for his decision. Even the right-wing *Daily Telegraph*, hardly a model of diverse opinion but owned by a rival media tycoon, spoke eloquently in defense of Proffitt and Patten. The book was moved to an alternative publishing house and Proffitt ended up in another excellent publishing job; in this case the story had a happy ending.

Generally, it is safe to say that whenever a conglomerate has a wide variety of holdings, there is a very real risk that its media companies will not report news that might diminish the profitability of other branches of the firm. In France, for instance, the Hachette group has long been part of a large corporation that also owns much of the French armament industry. To my knowledge, no major critiques of the arms trade have been published by Hachette, nor are there likely to be.

When Putnam was briefly owned by a major Japanese electronics firm, its president came to the United States on an inaugural visit. He had not been briefed on the ways of the American press and so answered with unexpected frankness when one of the reporters asked if Putnam would publish material critical of Japan's behavior during the war. Evidently surprised by what he took to be a silly question, he replied that of course they would not. Since books critical of Japan's behavior during the war have had a very hard time being published in Japan itself, why would overseas subsidiaries be allowed to put them out? The broader the holdings of conglomerates, the more likely it is that these forms of internal censorship will increase.

Only twice during my long years at Pantheon were we pressured not to publish a book for political reasons. One was a book on Arab-Israeli relations by the French Islamicist, Maxim Rodinson. Rodinson was a highly respected scholar, but his views were at odds with those of some of the more militant advocates of Israel, including George Weidenfeld, the British publisher. Unbeknownst to me, Weidenfeld protested our publishing the book to Bob Bernstein, who, to his credit, passed Weidenfeld's letter directly to me. No further obstacles were placed in the book's way and *Israel and the Arabs* was published in 1969.

The other case was more serious. Pantheon had taken on a young Chilean exile named Ariel Dorfman, then little known in the United States. Dorfman had published a very clever illustrated critique of Disney, which had been prevented from circulating in the United States by Disney's watchful copyright lawyers. The book we wanted to publish, *The Empire's New Clothes*, was similarly pointed about Disney comics. Since the text was not illustrated, there was no question of a lawsuit, but the criticism of Disney caused great anxiety in Random House's juvenile department — then the foremost publisher of Disney properties. The department's head protested vigorously to Bob Bernstein that our book would be harmful to their relationship with Disney. The book's editor, Tom Engelhardt, and I both felt that the issue was one of basic principle and decided that we would resign if the book were blocked — but we did not tell Bob this. I remember sitting with Tom in Bob's anteroom, nervously wondering what would happen and ready to announce our departure if needed. As it turned out, we had overestimated the danger, since Bob had no intention of bowing to such pressure. Neither Ariel nor Bob ever knew of our decision, and I suspect Bob would have laughed at us had he heard of it. He was to become a major advocate of the First Amendment and a strong supporter of dissident writing, particularly in the Soviet Union. He subsequently founded Human Rights Watch, which he has continued to lead since his departure from Random House.

Publishing on political issues, particularly around elections, was for many years characteristic of American publishing houses. But in both the 1992 and 1996 presidential campaigns, virtually no books were published for the general reader that dealt with the big issues facing American citizens. NAFTA, health insurance, the future of the welfare system — such topics were rarely discussed in books other than those that took a markedly right-wing position. These books were often subsidized by right-wing foundations and published by major conglomerates. There is no question in my mind that some of the more controversial issues, such as NAFTA and national health care, would have been dealt with very differently had a public discussion been fostered by critical books at the time.

In a survey in 1996, *Publishers Weekly* listed some forty new political books, all backing Gingrich and the right and just one dissenting title — which The New Press published. The major houses have pretty much abandoned well-argued left-of-center books, which are now the preserve of a few independent and alternative houses.

⁓

IF THE TRANSFORMATION of commercial publishing is as extensive as I've described, can university presses provide an alternative? Many of them have pinned their hopes on publishing the midlist books that the conglomerates are abandoning, making money for themselves while rescuing important books from oblivion. The situation, however, has turned out to be more complicated. The not-for-profit sector has been subjected to increasing commercial pressures, which have in some cases amounted to de facto privatization.

It was inevitable that corporate approaches would eventually hit the university presses. After all, were not whole academic departments being closed down for lack of customers? If the teaching process itself was under the influence of such pressures, what fire wall was there to protect the university presses?

In an article in the *Times Literary Supplement* last year that provoked widespread discussion in England, including debate in the House of Lords, Sir Keith Thomas raised the question of what university presses can do best in today's marketplace. Thomas, a well-known historian, is head of the Oxford University Press finance committee and one of those responsible for Oxford's decision to discontinue the publication of contemporary poetry. His article was, in some respects, disingenuous. He described Oxford as a middle-sized publisher, when its annual global sales of close to half a billion dollars make it a giant in its class. Oxford's sales are greater than all of the American university presses put together. The Oxford list includes a large number of highly commercial books, and their extensive trade publishing contributes significantly to profits. Thomas also stated that Oxford University is entitled to "a reasonable return" from its press which, over the last five years, has paid back to the university an average of $16 million each year. In light of this, the move to cut back on poetry seemed mean and philistine to many critics.

Further cutbacks at Oxford also eliminated the intellectually important paperback series Opus, the Modern Masters series, and the use of Clarendon Press as a meaningful imprint. Letters in the pages of the *TLS*, some from former OUP employees, expressed anger about Oxford's decisions. The barbarians were no longer at the gate, it was argued, they were well entrenched in Oxford's management.

In defense of these closures Thomas invoked familiar changes: the increased concentration of the ownership of publishing houses and of bookstores, the subsequent profit pressure on publishers who find themselves giving ever higher discounts to the chains, the difficulty of competing in a nearly monopolized market. These questions are pressing for a publisher the size of Oxford, less so for the smaller American university presses. But the issue raised by Oxford University Press about making a profit to pay its owners is something many of those in the university sector now have to face.

It is clear that, like Oxford, American university presses are suffering because of how much it costs to publish monographs, traditionally their major output. In a thoughtful article for the *New York Review of Books*, Professor Robert Darnton argued convincingly for the publication of monographs on-line, citing dwindling sales (which can now be as low as 200 copies) and the crisis in libraries, whose funds are increasingly diverted to learned journals. (These are also all but monopolized and a single journal can now cost up to $16,000 per year.)

But at the same time as their principal "product" — the monograph — is proving ever more expensive, support from universities is diminishing. According to Thomas, nearly all American university presses receive subsidies from their owners, but in fact an increasing number are now expected to break even or make a profit. Ohio State University, for instance, recently demanded 7 percent of its press's sales, though that number was later negotiated down. After a singularly successful year, the University of New Mexico Press found itself hit with a 10 percent tax by its university. The University of Chicago, true to its economic teaching, considers the whole university a profit center, and demands of each of its departments — including the press — an annual increase in profitability. We are told that young accountants scurry about the campus every quarter, asking department heads whether they have made the progress expected of them in their business plan, a ritual familiar to anyone who has worked in corporate America. A recent internal study of forty-nine university presses showed that over the last four years, their annual subsidy from universities had decreased by 8 percent in real dollars, and that twelve presses lost over 10 percent of their support.

To use the elegant phrase of Peter Givler, head of the Association of American University Presses, many universities can be said to be offering "negative support."

In my discussions with university press directors I was surprised by their reluctance to speak for attribution. They were happy to talk about what was happening in other presses, but often unwilling to be quoted directly. Here, too, the chilling climate of a large corporation could be felt, rather than the spirit of open inquiry, which is supposed to characterize university dealings.

If the role of monographs diminishes in the coming years and university support continues to decline, where are university presses to turn? For some time now, a number have tried to become regional publishers as a solution to this dilemma. Presses such as Nebraska and Oklahoma have developed impressive lines of books on local history. In areas that have no independent local publishing, such a move clearly renders a valuable service.

Others have turned to the commercial world. Princeton University Press, the best endowed university press in the country, with an income of $23 million at its disposal, has been aggressive in trying to replace traditional monographs with more popular, commercially attractive titles. The space for serious publishing has been reduced by this approach. One of Walter Lippincott's first moves on arriving as director at Princeton in 1986 was to try to close down the Bollingen series (moved there from Pantheon when we were bought by Random House on the grounds that a nonprofit university press was a more appropriate home). Happily, Princeton's board recoiled at the suggestion.

Their recent catalogs suggest that many university presses have now devoted a substantial part of their programs to more commercial midlist titles, in the hope of covering their costs.[30] A surprisingly large number have turned to baseball as a subject worth covering; books about movie stars also proliferate. The current list of the University of California Press features a revised edition of Antonia Fraser's *History of the British Monarchy*, the kind of popular history that used to be published by Knopf. This reliance on books that commercial publishers have abandoned raises serious questions. Of course, it is not clear that these books can be sufficiently profitable in today's book-selling environment and many university presses have discovered that the market for midlist publishing is unreliable. But even when such books do make money, is it proper for a university press to be publishing them? Hundreds of millions of taxpayer dollars have been spent on such presses over the years, either directly or indirectly, through tax-exempt alumni contributions. This money was meant to insure that the presses remain a source of scholarship and information, one of the few available to the country as a whole.

Looking at the writing on the wall for university presses, I think I can make out the letters "PBS." Public television was subjected to major political pressure during the Reagan-Bush years, during which period government funding was deliberately removed in order to force broadcasters to seek private sponsorship and to ensure anodyne, less politically confrontational programming. The decline of public television is another example of what happens when the market becomes the arbiter of what is to be made available. The search for wider audiences will invariably dilute educational content. If the university presses choose to follow the lure of the trade-book market, we may well see a similar evolution there.

As I mentioned previously, I once had the opportunity to appear before the search committee of Harvard University Press to discuss its future publishing. I prepared a long and detailed memo. Acknowledging that Harvard was already preeminent in the publication of scholarly work and monographs, I suggested that the press devote some of its efforts — and profits — to other areas. Noting that John Silber, the ultra-conservative president of Boston University, was making energetic attempts to take over the Boston city schools, I suggested that Harvard consider directing some of its expertise in the field of education toward publishing books for teachers and students in the Boston area. I also proposed that Harvard pay more attention to scholarly publishing overseas, helping fledgling university presses in Eastern Europe and in the Third World through translations and cocommissioning.

Had I suggested to the distinguished committee that we march down to Harvard Yard and set the Widener Library ablaze, I would have made a better impression. It was clear that Harvard saw its role as publishing for only its faculty and their peers in the university world. It was not part of its agenda to concern itself with the needs of local schools. But Massachusetts, like all states, has high school courses in state history. Thanks to the local AFL-CIO, its legislature even recently approved a requirement in local labor history. These areas are not being met at a high intellectual and scholarly standard by the commercial textbook houses and could have been a worthy challenge for a university press.

TAKEN TOGETHER, what remains of the independent sector in publishing—the university presses, the nonprofits, the church-owned houses, and the presses associated with major foundations—can still play an important role. But the playing field is anything but level, and the resources available are too limited.

The Bowker data bank of publishing houses lists a mind-boggling fifty-three thousand publishers in the country. But this number must be kept in perspective. Remember: 93 percent of annual sales are controlled by the top twenty firms, another 2 percent by the hundred-plus university presses. All of 5 percent of book sales are left to be fought over by this vast number of publishers. Nor does being small and independent guarantee publishing at the highest level. The vast majority of the small firms are publishers of how-to books, religious and inspirational books, regional guides, and the like.

However, this growing band of independents also includes a number of small literary houses like Copper Canyon, Milkweed, Coffeehouse, Graywolf, Seven Stories, and Four Walls Eight Windows, who have taken on the publishing of serious fiction, poetry, and political thought. Without their presence, it would be impossible for many beginning authors to find an audience.

Another source of independent publishing is the churches who have for years supported their own houses, some purely centered around denominational interests, some seeking to reach a broader audience. Among these, firms such as Beacon Press, Orbis, and Pilgrim have intervened in political debate and offered ethical discourse. Such presses played an essential role opposing the Vietnam War, for instance.

Because of the marked lack of books from commercial firms on political and social issues, there has also been a significant increase in publishing by foundations seeking an audience for research they have funded. On the right, the Heritage Press and the Cato Institute have grown in importance, partly taking over the role that was once played by The Free Press. The right-wing Bradley Foundation, based in Milwaukee, recently gave $3 million to polemicist Peter Collier to start a new house, Encounter (which many will remember as the name of the CIA-funded journal that played an important role in postwar Britain). At the center-left of the political spectrum, the Brookings Institute and the Century Foundation (formerly the Twentieth-Century Fund) have become increasingly important in funding publishing. These presses are very much the heirs to the New Deal and Fair Deal years, publishing the kinds of studies that are close to the hearts of liberal democrats, books that once were published in large numbers by the houses now owned by the conglomerates. In addition, there are still a handful of independent political publishers, which include Regnery on the right — the continuation of the Henry Regnery firm that was a leading right-wing publisher in the 1950s—and a number of publishers on the left such as Monthly Review, South End, Common Courage, and others.

Another important source of questioning, critical publishing comes from the few remaining trade houses that continue to work in the spirit of openness and respect for broad audiences that was once standard in America. Notable among these is W. W. Norton (the distributor for The New Press), both for its list and for its unusual structure. It is the only large firm that is owned by its executives, an arrangement established when the firm was founded over seventy-five years ago. This is a strong deterrent to outside firms who might have tried to take it over and it has served Norton well. But Norton is more than an independent firm. The quality of its books has not diminished over the years and its titles earn more reviews and literary prizes every year. There are a number of other trade publishers, such as Harcourt Brace, Houghton Mifflin, and the newly established Metropolitan Books at Henry Holt, that, while being owned by conglomerates, have managed to retain intellectual independence and are still able to publish works of high caliber. In most of these cases, the trade lists are only a small part of a much larger textbook business whose owners presumably want to retain the cachet of an intellectually respected trade presence.

A promising experiment has begun with Perseus Books. Headed by a former HarperCollins executive and funded by a consortium of banks, Perseus has pursued the clever strategy of buying up houses just as they are dumped by conglomerates. Familiar with the economics of the Murdoch holdings, Perseus took over Basic Books and Westview Publishers, both formerly owned by Harper's, as well as Counterpoint, a reincarnation of the distinguished North Point imprint, which had previously been owned by Random House. New lists have also been launched, including Public Affairs, headed by Peter Osnos, the former Random House vice president. Today Perseus publishes 350 books a year with sales of $65 million, an impressive if risky beginning since trying to outbid conglomerates is an expensive proposition.

Two different examples, one American, the other French, provide hope and stand as models for further experimentation. Dalkey

Archive, named after one of Flann O'Brien's lesser-known novels, is based in the unlikely venue of Normal, Illinois. It is located there because its staff is on the faculty at the local State University of Illinois and the firm uses university offices and works with graduate students. Its director is a tenured professor, freed of teaching duties so that he can devote time to the press. The house has developed one of the more interesting lists in American literary publishing, making available a wide range of important works, both in translation and in English. In addition to Flann O'Brien, Dalkey has published the novellas of Arno Schmidt and the novels of Nicholas Mosley, which, though demanding, have become unexpected commercial successes. Dalkey has pieced together out of bits of free space and free time a model that could easily be emulated at universities throughout the country. There is no reason why university presses should not encourage ancillary alternative publishing houses that could share their facilities and publish in areas that the university is wary of venturing into. University presses have barely scratched the surface of what should be translated or, equally important, what could be reissued. Such publishing houses could fill the growing gap in our knowledge of thinking abroad and writing in the past.

An equally inspiring example can be found in France on a larger scale, in one of the most exciting and promising of recent developments in European publishing. Pierre Bourdieu's *Raisons d'agir* (Reasons to Act) series consists of small, inexpensive books, published from his office in the Collège de France. These books have dominated French best-seller lists with their new ideas, polemics, and criticism. While other French publishers have increasingly shied away from radical publishing, Bourdieu has plunged into the field. The series comprises short, controversial books sold for less than ten dollars, a very low price in the French market. As a result, some of his titles have sold over 100,000 copies. Their tremendous sales can be attributed in part to Bourdieu's own growing reputation, but they are also the result of a publishing strategy that appeals especially to a younger audience generally ignored by other publishers. Bourdieu, a brilliant critic of the media, has found a way of intervening in public debate that is free from the constraints of traditional publishing.

We know from history that experimentation and discovery are far more likely to take place on a smaller scale where risks can be taken and enthusiasms pursued. As Klaus Wagenbach, the noted German publisher and Kafka scholar, wrote recently:

> Independent publishers are once again disappearing into the grasping arms of the same two conglomerates. You may ask, is that so bad? Let me explain briefly why it's not just bad — it's disastrous.
>
> Let's imagine the future. What if, in this brave new future, there are only a handful of publishing houses left, like, say, in the former East Germany. What is — not thinking in terms of communism and capitalism here — attractive about that? That books will be cheaper? Maybe. But only a tenth as many will be published at all. In East Germany, this was because of Party censorship. In our hypothetical future, it will be because of censorship imposed by the tastes of the mass market.
>
> Big houses think in terms of big numbers.
>
> But new, strange, crazy, intellectually innovative, or experimental books are published in small to medium-size print runs. That is the task of the smaller houses. Ourselves. These smaller houses are not made up of marketing experts. They are staffed by people who

do books because of their passion or their strong opinions — certainly not because of the profits they will generate. Books that otherwise would not be published at all.

Let's make this as explicit as possible: If books with small print runs disappear, the future will die. Kafka's first book was published with a printing of 800 copies. Brecht's first work merited 600. What would have happened if someone had decided that was not worth it?[31]

⁓

WE CANNOT SPEAK of open competition or a free market in American publishing today. We are faced with a classic situation of oligopoly, approaching monopoly. The conglomerates' links, through common ownership, to other media give them incredible advantages in press, television, and newspaper coverage and publicity. Firms that own publishing houses as well as magazines have not hesitated to give a disproportionate amount of attention to books emanating from the companies they control. The changes that are needed to deal with this kind of power are obvious. The most effective solution to the increasing conglomeratization is in the hands of the government. Unfortunately, in the United States and Britain, as we have seen, conglomerates' control of key media is so powerful that governments have been afraid to invoke the provisions of antitrust legislation.

Some promising developments have occurred in the European Union. A recent decision of the EU antimonopoly commission blocked the proposed merger of Reed Elsevier with Wolter Kluwer, two originally Dutch but now international conglomerates that control a large percentage of the reference and information world, as we have seen. The commission rightly decided that this merger would have given these two firms a near monopoly in crucial fields. It is hoped that European governments, increasingly aware of the fact that their national cultural independence is being threatened by such conglomerates, will prevent further mergers and even question those already in place.

A second possible solution is technological. Much has been made of the value of the Internet as a method for disseminating information. With limited capital and minimal training, anyone can establish a Web site, any author can publish his or her work, any journal can begin publishing and perhaps reach a like-minded audience throughout the world. But clearly the amount of material presently on-line is as much a problem as it is an opportunity. How can we know if what is offered is reliable? In this very question we see the advantage of the publishing system. Publishers, above all, are people who make a selection, who choose and edit material that will be distributed according to certain criteria, and then market and publicize it. By putting their name to writers' work, they provide a guarantee and guide to the reader.

Further, the idea that the Internet automatically provides a democratic way to propagate information is by no means proven. Very few sites have discovered how to get visitors to pay for the material they have access to, and while getting on the Internet is relatively easy, establishing and maintaining a site that will attract an audience is an expensive venture involving substantial design and advertising budgets. There is every reason to assume that larger firms, with greater marketing clout, will dominate the

Internet in the same way they have asserted themselves in more conventional publishing. They may also ultimately control our access to that medium.

Stephen King recently published a novella on the Internet. The extraordinary success of this experiment has sparked the imagination of authors and publishers alike. Several hundred thousand copies of the book were sold on the first day; the site received so many hits that it was overwhelmed by them. This has led many to speculate on the end of publishing as we know it. They foresee a system for distributing books very similar to the one being developed by the music industry, where content is sent out over the Internet and downloaded by the customer.

However, the results of King's initiative suggest that distribution on the Web may be most effective, at least at first, on the extremes of the publishing spectrum. As mentioned, there has been considerable discussion about the possible distribution of academic monographs — books that would normally sell at most 350 copies and whose audience is easily targeted on the Web. The other end of the publishing spectrum, work by best-selling authors who have a ready-made audience and a proven track record, may also do well on the Web. In these cases money for widespread advertising and marketing will be available and an impatient readership will want to have the book on the day it appears.

The fear that best-selling authors might publish their own work has haunted the conglomerates for many years now. It is only through substantial overpayment that conglomerates have managed to keep the loyalty of many of them. They know that the Stephen Kings of this world can easily hire a printer and a distributor. Now with the advent of the Internet, that threat is all the more apparent. In a recent series of lectures at the New York Public Library, Jason Epstein raised this specter, but without drawing the obvious conclusions. With conglomerates becoming dependent on the sales of leading titles, will they still be willing to publish the rest of their lists if those "locomotives" disappear into the Internet? The change of intention in the large publishers from publishing a wide range of books to focusing on profit-maximization suggests that their whole enterprise may be at far greater risk than Epstein is willing to admit. The Internet may well accelerate the process we have been considering. Whether it will be of equal use to the authors and publishers of smaller books that do not merit the massive advertising required by Internet sites is another question. As we know from the huge advertising budgets of e-commerce firms, much more money is needed to launch a site successfully than to publish a year's worth of books in a small publishing house. The technological wonders of the Internet may not be enough to challenge the profit-making structures that are now in place.

Innovations in the means of communication, from the advent of radio and television to the Web, are often accompanied by a wave of optimism at the outset, suggesting that, this time, the new machines will be used wisely and effectively to help build networks of educational value and cultural uplift. These illusions dissipate quickly. Whether the Internet and its many investors will choose a different path is yet to be seen.

A third possibility for change is that governments directly provide help to publishers as part of a broader program of assistance to cultural institutions. Many European governments now have substantial aid policies for filmmakers. There are also new cross-national associations such as the publicly subsidized French-German television station Arte, which broadcasts at a level higher than anything that can be seen in the English-speaking world or, indeed, in most of Europe. Why shouldn't book production warrant similar public help?

While there is a history of governmental assistance for publishing in Europe as part of a concerted attempt to create national policies to support both book-selling and publishing, there have been few parallel efforts in the United States. Most of what little public support for publishing in America exists has been channeled through the NEA and the NEH, but today both are very much on the defensive. Because of massive funding cuts in recent years, they have sharply reduced the amount granted to publishers to help make scholarly and innovative work available. Only a few major projects — the collected works of central figures in American history, for example — continue to receive this kind of aid. Still, it is not impossible to at least imagine the creation of a significant endowment funded by the existing governmental entities — the NEA, the NEH, and the Museum Institute. Such a plan could have a substantial impact. A great deal of interesting work is generated by the research grants given out by these organizations, and very little of it ever sees the light of day. The large amounts of federal money spent on developing new curricula, funding research and translation, and generating new museum programs is wasted if the results are not published. A more enlightened Congress might be persuaded about this.

The New Press has taken on a number of high-school-level science education projects developed by the Museum of Natural

History in New York and the Exploratorium in San Francisco but hundreds of valuable educational endeavors such as these are going unpublished. Commercial publishers find them insufficiently profitable; university presses are, for the most part, uninterested in school-age readers.

Beyond such obvious projects, there is a great deal of additional work worthy of federal support. Institutions have given substantial grants for the translation of foreign literature and scholarship for years, but help could also be given in funding the publication of such translations. A publishing endowment could help distribute books to the country's public libraries, whose budgets have been so severely depleted lately. For a small amount of money, libraries and schools could bring their readers a far wider choice than is now available.

Clearly, such proposals are not at the top of anyone's agenda today. The problems that face us all at the century's beginning are overwhelming both in their magnitude and in their complexity. But if the domain of ideas is surrendered to those who want to make the most money, then the debate that is so essential for a functioning democracy will not take place. To a large degree it is this silence that has overtaken much of American intellectual life.

Books today have become mere adjuncts to the world of the mass media, offering light entertainment and reassurances that all is for the best in this, the best of all possible worlds. The resulting control on the spread of ideas is stricter than anyone would have thought possible in a free society. The need for public debate and open discussion, inherent in the democratic ideal, conflicts with the ever-stricter demand for total profit.

Robert McChesney, in his valuable book, *Rich Media, Poor Democracy*, quotes from the debate that took place in the 1930s over whether radio should be delivered entirely into private hands or maintain an independent, nonprofit base:

> Freedom of speech is the very foundation of democracy. To allow private interests to monopolize the most powerful means of reaching the human mind is to destroy democracy. Without freedom of speech, without honest presentation of facts by people whose primary interest is *not* profits, there can be no intelligent basis for the determination of public policy.[32]

SIX

The New Press

WHEN WE all left Pantheon at the beginning of 1990, it was clear that a new solution to the problems we had faced in publishing needed to be found. But it would take time for us to assess the lessons of other independent presses and decide what to do next. My colleagues needed to find work immediately and could not afford the luxury of waiting for the development of a new structure. Much to my sorrow, the group that had worked so well together at Pantheon dispersed.

As for me, exploratory offers of work began to come in from investment bankers and publishers in the weeks following our departure. My old colleague at Basic Books, Martin Kessler, called to ask if I would consider setting up a similar imprint at Harper's, linked to Basic. Basic was one of the few remaining firms whose output I respected, but their future under Murdoch seemed uncertain. Much as I appreciated Martin's proposal, I felt that we might be making a trip from the proverbial frying pan into the fire, and I refused. How quickly the fire was to burn surprised even me. Within months, Martin was forced out of Basic, to work briefly, until his untimely death, at The Free Press. Basic itself was to prove equally vulnerable.

For many years, I had felt that the country needed a new kind of publisher, a book equivalent to PBS and NPR. Clearly, this was a once-in-a-lifetime chance to see if this theory could be put into practice. I greatly admired Bill Moyers's work in setting up the alternative broadcasting networks. But by 1990 these had been weakened. PBS in particular, under pressure from Washington, had started abandoning more and more of its political and social broadcasts, replacing them with an anodyne mix of antique road shows, nostalgic celebrations of local and ethnic history, and endless culinary programs. The experience of PBS, as well as the culture wars that were raging around the NEA at the time, made me wary of pursuing government funding. It seemed unrealistic to expect to be encouraged to publish critical political books and countercyclical analyses at a time when Congress was eager to eliminate any trace of dissidence among its grantees. (After close to ten years of existence, The New Press has received less than 0.5 percent of its outside support from governmental entities.)

This left only two possible approaches. One was to find a good-hearted millionaire who would be willing to back us, as James Laughlin had funded New Directions in the 1920s or Paul Mellon had the Bollingen Foundation in the 1950s. But that seemed highly wishful, akin to waiting for Santa Claus to descend our chimney. A more realistic option was to turn to foundations. We could make a good case for creating an alternative medium to deal with the political and social issues being neglected by conglomerate publishers. We intended to focus on many of the social issues on which foundations had spent billions in research and other grants. It was logical that a publisher devoted to such issues might be worthy of their support.

A major problem with this approach was that many of the large foundations had already tried to support new ventures in publishing over the years, largely by helping existing commercial houses take on books that they would have otherwise ignored and often at exorbitant cost. Even Random House occasionally announced an unlikely title backed by tens of thousands of foundation dollars. As I approached several foundations, I found that their reservations were considerable. Maybe this would not be the right route after all.

Then, by good fortune, I came across two foundation executives who understood exactly what we were attempting to do. Colin Campbell, the head of the Rockefeller Brothers Fund, had been president of Wesleyan College and, as such, he was familiar with the problems publishers were facing. He was the first to offer help and he gave us a crucial list of colleagues to approach at other foundations. Woody Wickham, who was in charge of grants to the media at the MacArthur Foundation, was another person who saw the merit of our proposal. Happily, MacArthur became our first major funder, giving us a million dollars over our first four years, a sum that made The New Press possible; they continued to support us thereafter. Campbell contributed a smaller amount of money but provided essential support, along with Richard Leone, head of the then Twentieth-Century Fund, by arranging a lunch to which a dozen foundation executives agreed to come. I prepared my presentation for this meeting over several months, joking that this was the most important sales conference I had ever attended. In many ways the process was analogous. I needed to persuade a group of sympathetic but skeptical people that the project we had drawn up on paper would succeed in the real world. Of the dozen executives present, ten eventually persuaded their foundations to support us.

The total amount of money we were looking for was not large by foundation standards. It came to well under a million dollars the first year, less than 1 percent of what New York's PBS outlet, Channel Thirteen, raises every year. But this was sufficient to pay for the publication of the books we had in manuscript and the remainder of the books we planned to publish in this first year. Once these books were sold, enough money would come in to allow us to publish our next list and so on, hopefully into perpetuity.

More unexpected support came to us from the late Joe Murphy, then chancellor of City University. Joe, a political scientist, was a good friend of Fran Piven, one of Pantheon's most important authors, and later the chair of our board of directors. He had followed the Pantheon story with interest, and shortly after I left the company he came up with a very generous offer. He was about to leave his post as chancellor and had moved to an office in a neglected CUNY building on Forty-first Street, west of the Port Authority Terminal. His wife, the artist Susan Crile, taught art students there as part of the Hunter College MFA program. He wanted to be near her and he enjoyed teaching the often untutored artists some basic lessons in political thinking. Joe had already invited Alan Lomax, the great 1930s ethnomusicologist, whose memoir we had commissioned at Pantheon, to be his neighbor. A new CUNY university press was about to be launched and it shared the same floor. But there was still some empty space and Joe offered it to us, free of charge.

We couldn't have hoped for more concrete help. Public support without the risk of any threat to our First Amendment rights was theoretically impossible, and yet here it was, offered without our even having asked for it. We accepted with alacrity and I went with Joe to examine the new quarters we were to share. I had dreamed of a small brownstone in the Village or perhaps a top floor with a few offices devoted to The Press, like what we had in our early days at Pantheon. I certainly wasn't prepared for the appearance of the CUNY building. Once the site of Voorhees Technical College, it was decrepit and dilapidated. We went up the rickety elevator to the expansive offices that formed the core of Joe's domain. There was no possibility of a discrete entrance or separate quarters. We were offered two contiguous offices on a long corridor shared with a number of other tenants, including a program for retraining workers for the MTA. Much as I liked the idea of being identified with CUNY and grateful as I was to Joe, my face fell when I saw the dusty rooms in front of me. I hoped that Joe had not noticed my disappointment, but he was so enthusiastic about the surrounding neighborhood that I think he paid no attention to it. And of course he was right. The offices could be made to work and there was plenty of room for expansion. The neighborhood rents were as low as you could get in central New York and the grocery stores nearby sold their treasures at a fraction of what I was used to paying near my home on the Upper West Side. Joe delighted in pointing out the bargain prices for fresh swordfish, plum tomatoes, and delicacies from Africa and Latin America. I found myself taking home food parcels more days than not, an unexpected bonus to our new location.

The next key element was to find someone to sell our books. Our choices were limited. We were not about to go to one of the conglomerates. We wanted an independent publisher, preferably one in New York whose books were similar to ours. The choice was soon narrowed down to two candidates. Roger Straus III was an ex-colleague and a friend who had expressed interest in the possibility of Farrar, Straus & Giroux distributing our list. At the same time, I approached Donald Lamm, the head of W. W. Norton, whose list was in many ways the closest to what we were planning both in the level of its books and its commitment to independence. In addition, Norton was known for its strength at the college level and indeed for years had been carried by the profitability of its well-known textbooks. Since we hoped that many of our books would in time be assigned as part of college curricula, we finally chose Norton. (That turned out to be just as well, since Roger soon broke with his father, the head of Farrar, Straus &Giroux, who was much less enthusiastic about taking us on.)

I went to Norton's sales conference shortly after we signed our agreement, before we even had any books of our own to present. It was an extraordinary reminder of my first days at Pantheon. A dozen salespeople were gathered around a wooden table in a midtown hotel, listening to presentations of a list of titles, very similar to the ones that Knopf had been publishing when I first joined Random House. It was as if we were in a time machine going back thirty years to a publishing world that was far simpler, more straightforward, and honest. I immediately felt at home.

With offices and a distributor in place and having begun to look for funding, we now had to find editors and authors. When we left Pantheon, I had urged my younger colleagues to stay put because I felt it would not be easy for them to find jobs elsewhere. One of those who remained behind was Diane Wachtell, my former assistant. Despite pressure to stay with Random House, Diane agreed to sign on as our first paid employee and later became — and remains — our associate director. Working under the enormous pressure of our first years, she displayed a remarkable range of talents, administrative and financial as well as editorial. Her collaboration has been an essential part of The New Press's success, and her editorial skills have been central in helping to shape some of our most important books. We were soon joined by two others: Dawn Davis, a brilliant young woman who had been a trainee at First Boston until she decided that there was more to life than banking, and came to be my assistant; and David Sternbach, another of Pantheon's young assistant editors, who joined us briefly as a part-time editor.

Another crucial offer of help came from Tony Schulte, who had been vice president at Random House in charge of trade, and with whom I had worked closely over the years. Tony left Random House before all the changes and had set up as an adviser on mergers and acquisitions in publishing. He hardly needed the money, nor did he need the aggravation of once again having to worry about the financial cares of a small publisher. But I badly wanted his advice and help, and I knew that his being with us would answer the many questions that would arise concerning the kind of financial guidance we had on board. Tony generously agreed to work for us, helping to guide us through our first perilous years, and ultimately joining our board of directors.

Diane, Dawn, David, and I began to put together our first list, modest in size, including several titles that we had been able to salvage from Pantheon. "Salvage" was a word I found myself using frequently; we were like Robinson Crusoe on his desert island. But on rereading the childhood classic I discovered that Crusoe had survived not simply through his own ingenuity but by means of the precious objects that he had been able to bring in from the ship, which, for the sake of the book's plot, took a very long time to sink. As essential as the shovels and nails (and bottles of rum) that Crusoe managed to bring to his island were the manuscripts that our authors had been holding for us during the year that followed our departure from Pantheon. It was an act of faith for authors to wait like this, particularly when, as in Studs Terkel's case, very substantial offers were being made by other publishers. But Studs, Edward Thompson, Marguerite Duras, John Dower, Lucy Lippard, Ada Louise Huxtable, Foucault's heirs, and many others we would have published at Pantheon were unstinting in their support and waited until we had raised the money needed to get out their books. This allowed us to produce a first catalog that included several major titles that we knew would attract the attention of both reviewers and bookstores and establish The New Press as a substantial publisher. Studs's book *Race: How Blacks and Whites Think and Feel about the American Obsession* appeared just as the riots consumed Los Angeles; it became an instant best-seller. Of the hundreds of authors we'd published at Pantheon, only three opted to stay with Random House.

In time we discovered that we could sell substantial quantities of meaningful, intellectual titles, including those that no one in the commercial world thought would ever find an audience. We were also encouraged by all the important social science writers who were willing to come to us from commercial publishers, authors such as John Womack, Jorge Castañeda, Vincent Crapanzano, and Katherine Newman.

Our initial foundation backers have since been joined by close to fifty others in providing the small proportion of The New Press's budget not generated through book sales. That support acts as the publishing equivalent of old-style scholarships in higher education. Books are admitted according to merit, not for their potential contribution to the bottom line. Now in its eighth year, The New Press has been able to publish well over three hundred books, ranging from translations of foreign literature to demanding works of legal theory and history to arguments for countercyclical political ideas (where established houses fear to tread).

During our planning year, when we tried to raise the initial funds needed to launch the press and worked on the manuscripts that we already had in hand, we had ample time to look back at what we had done at Pantheon and to see what its strengths and weaknesses were. As I was already in my midfifties, I felt strongly that this was my last chance to get things right. I was proud of what had been achieved at Pantheon, but I realized that there were a number of areas that could be improved upon. For instance, the Pantheon staff, with only the rarest of exceptions, was all white and middle class. In that respect we were typical of the rest of Random House, whose baseball team was made up primarily of people from the mailroom.

At The New Press we resolved to make every effort to have as diverse a staff as possible, as well as having a board of directors that would act as a link to the country's different intellectual and political constituencies.

We soon discovered that it was fruitless to try to recruit minority personnel from elsewhere in publishing. There were so few people that there seemed little point in moving them from one place to another. Remembering the sustained effort the industry had made in the 1960s to hire minority personnel, it was shocking to see how few were employed in today's companies.

The only solution possible was to look outside. After Dawn Davis joined us, another black editor arrived from the *Village Voice*. Until his tragic disappearance in the summer of 1999, in what is presumed to be a hiking accident, Joe Wood made an immeasurable contribution to The New Press. An accomplished writer, Joe proved to be one of the ablest and most intelligent editors I have ever worked with. Though he had no previous experience in book publishing, he played a vital role, both in finding African-American authors and in discovering important research on various aspects of American history, race, and politics. Joe's success in the three years that he worked with us showed how much more could be achieved in publishing by looking beyond the usual channels.

In time, our modest effort at minority recruitment would be seen as a model by the publishing industry and became the subject of various magazine articles and interviews. I found myself asked to advise other publishers, far richer and better placed than we, how they might make a greater effort to diversify their staffs. Even university presses, in campuses filled with bright young people of color, seemed to have great difficulty finding minority staff or even interns. There are real problems to be faced in this area, such as the miserably low salaries paid in publishing as a whole, especially at the entry level, which makes it difficult for young people without at least some parental financial support to get into the industry. But The New Press's success has shown that if a determined effort is made in this direction, such difficulties can at least be confronted, if not completely resolved.

～

WE DECIDED to form a series of advisory committees composed of scholars and teachers from fields such as law, education, and civil rights to help us identify gaps in the literature and potential authors in a way that our small staff could not. The advisory committees played an integral role in our early years, giving us a clear sense of areas where important new work was being undertaken and how we might reach future audiences.

It seemed to us that certain kinds of books — and readers — had been neglected even before the advent of conglomerate ownership of publishing houses. Understandably, in an industry that had — and still has — primarily white, middle-class employees and assumptions, broader, more diverse audiences are bound to be ignored. Among our first efforts were experimental projects designed to reach these readerships. For example, we published several books on art history aimed specifically at black readers. These were not costly coffee-table books geared to the middle classes, but inexpensive editions that could readily be purchased by people on modest budgets. For the most part, the books sold out their first printings of 7,500 copies within a few months.

It was not only minority audiences that had been underestimated. A general belief in the industry was that no substantial public existed for political books demanding intellectual effort. Soon after we began The New Press, a law professor named Peter Irons came to us. He had discovered that the bulk of spoken arguments before the United States Supreme Court had been recorded for more than forty years but that the tapes, sitting in the National Archives, had never been reproduced. We decided to publish a selection in a book-and-tape set, even though colleagues elsewhere in the business advised us that we could hope to reach only a very specialized audience; they recommended a first printing of not more than 5,000 copies. As it turned out, these books and tapes were among our first best-sellers. Sales were helped by publicity generated by the Chief Justice's initial opposition to their release and further boosted by the broadcast of some of the tapes on public radio. But the project could not have succeeded had not a great many people shown a deep interest in how the law is made and interpreted. More than 75,000 copies are now in print.

Similarly, in 1995, we were counseled to order only a small print run of James W. Loewen's long, detailed study comparing the twelve most widely used high school textbooks in American history. The author, whose history of Mississippi we had published at Pantheon, had a sharp pen, a good sense of humor, and an excellent title, *Lies My Teacher Told Me: Everything Your American History Textbook Got Wrong*. With book club adoptions and paperback editions for which we sold rights, there are now more than 350,000 copies of this title in print, demonstrating terrific interest in how and what we teach our children.

In addition, because a great deal of literary work from overseas was being ignored by large firms, it was not hard for us to find a promising group of young foreign authors. In our first year, we published five books of fiction and belles lettres from abroad, all of which appeared on the *Times*'s list of best books at the end of the year. One of them, Laurie Lee's *A Moment of War*, was among the top ten. In 1992, every author that we selected from our British colleagues' lists, Tibor Fischer, Romesh Gunesekera, and Abdulrazak Gurnah, appeared on the Booker Prize shortlist (a list that was severely criticized by some in London as being too "exotic" and "multicultural"). The success of our books in these areas did not so much reflect our editorial brilliance as the fact that we had an empty field largely to ourselves. The sales of translated fiction were increasingly limited, affected in large part by the decline in library budgets. Even a book that received good reviews in the *Times* and elsewhere might sell as few as 1,000 copies. No editor in a commercial firm could possibly defend such a publishing choice.

We also found that there were wide areas in nonfiction in which we would face little competition. I felt strongly that part of our focus should be on the new thinking that was taking place in the professions. Foucault, in his later years, began to despair of the political parties and suggested that it was among groups of professionals that the most useful and innovative approaches could be found. In my own experience, I discovered that while many of the people with whom we discussed politics felt anomie and uncertainty when confronting today's political process and particularly the existing parties, they had very clear ideas when it came to their professional lives. So we gathered a group of voluntary advisers in education, law, and medicine, who spent hours in our offices giving us advice both on the books they felt needed to be written and authors who might write them.

Even many of the university presses had decided that publishing in education was not a priority, perhaps because the books were deemed to be money losers, perhaps because the aura of a teacher's college was too lacking in prestige. From the beginning, we found it was not difficult to find valuable new authors in this field. One of our most rewarding discoveries was a MacArthur Award winner, Lisa Delpit, who had written a series of fascinating articles in the *Harvard Education Newsletter*. She wrote about the cultural conflict in the classroom between a teaching body that was largely white and a student population that was increasingly "other": 40 percent of America's schoolchildren at the time of writing are of non-European origin. Delpit's book, *Other People's Children*, became an extraordinary success, selling over 60,000 copies and helping us to attract a large number of younger scholars working on the problems now facing American educators. In law, we published a series of alternative textbooks focusing on some of the essential areas that were often neglected in the standard curriculum, including sexuality and the law and critical race theory. To our delight, the books became part of the curriculum at law schools throughout the country.

In 1998, we began to work with an impressive group of researchers who were documenting the effect of inequality on health issues such as life expectancy. In each case, we found ourselves involved with young and dynamic scholars, people I would have never had the opportunity to work with in traditional publishing, given the partitioning of publishing houses. Even at Pantheon, the idea of publishing books that might be used as textbooks in these fields would have been out of the question. But The New Press was small enough to be able to cross these barriers and concern itself with ideas rather than appropriate bureaucratic classifications.

The lesson we have drawn is that, although some types of books are undeniably harder to publish with every passing year, the audiences are there, untapped, simply because no one has tried to reach them. It has taken a nonprofit structure to discover those readers. While many editors in commercial houses would doubtless be delighted to experiment as we have, they are forced to concentrate on a handful of books that will allow them to meet the economic expectations of corporate owners. Many editors who have been around long enough to remember the times before conglomerates keenly regret the decimation of thoughtful publishing. People joining the ranks of publishing today have no such comparative vantage point. To them, the present situation is normal, and that is in itself a worrying development.

❧

IT WOULD BE foolish to see what has happened to publishing as a story with a happy ending in which small publishers and university presses pick up what large ones have forsaken and the free market shows once again that truth will out. Without undervaluing the work of The New Press and our colleagues in other independents, it must be emphasized that the resources we command are tiny compared to what any large conglomerate has. Together, we don't even come close to constituting 1 percent of the total sales in book publishing. We lack the money and personnel to compete seriously for space in bookstore chains and other venues that dominate today's book-selling. While some of us can boast the occasional windfall, more than 30 percent of all best-sellers in the last year have come from houses now under the Bertelsmann-Random House umbrella.

＋～＋

SOME MONTHS AGO I was asked to speak to a group of my Yale classmates as we celebrated the fortieth anniversary of our graduation. As might be expected, most of the people who showed up at New York's Yale club were affluent. Whether businessmen, lawyers, or doctors, they had done well in their careers.

I spoke about the changes that had taken place in publishing, and suggested that, as far as I knew, similar developments were occurring in all of what used to be known as the "liberal professions." Doctors complain that now they have to deal with money rather than with health, and wrestle with the pressures of HMOs, hospitals, and insurance companies to the point where their own decision-making is severely limited. Likewise, lawyers complain about the way their worth is measured by how much money they bring to the firm; even those earning over a million dollars a year deplore the diminution of their professional roles and freedom. Many academics speak bitterly of the profit pressures on campuses. Their departments are being closed, classes are being curtailed or eliminated, and issues decided according to market criteria — how much money will be produced through the activities of each department rather than how much knowledge or debate. After my talk, my former classmates concurred that their professions had been changed completely. Many began by saying, "I wouldn't want to start out in my career at this point," or "If I had known it was going to turn out this way, I might not have chosen to be . . ." whatever they had spent the last forty years doing.

The idea that our society has been fundamentally affected by the importance of money is widely recognized. Other values that have been looked to as countervailing forces are fast disappearing. Not only our belongings but our jobs and, indeed, our selves have become commodities to be bought and sold to the highest bidder. There have been other times in history when such changes have taken place. But now, linked to globalization and to the industrialization of the media, the effects are all the more staggering.

What has happened to the work of publishers is no worse than what has taken place in other liberal professions. But the change that has occurred in publishing is of paramount importance. It is only in books that arguments and inquiries can be conducted at length and in depth. Books have traditionally been the one medium in which two people, an author and an editor, could agree that something needed to be said, and for a relatively small amount of money, share it with the public. Books differ in crucial ways from other media. Unlike magazines, they are not advertiser-driven. Unlike television and films, they do not have to find a mass audience. Books can afford to go against the current, to raise new ideas, to challenge the status quo, in the hope that with time an audience will be found. The threat to such books and the ideas they contain—what used to be known as the marketplace of ideas — is a dangerous development not only for professional publishing, but for society as a whole. We need to find new ways of maintaining the discourse that used to be considered an essential part of a democratic society. The New Press and the other small publishers I've described have begun to deal with the challenge, but much more is required than what we've been able to accomplish so far. We must hope that in coming years more people, here and abroad, will realize how dangerous it is to live in a culture with a limited choice of ideas and alternatives, and how essential it is to maintain a wide-ranging debate. In short, to remember how important books have always been in our lives.

Notes

1   *Publishers Weekly*, December 12, 1998.

2   *Bertelsmann Newsletter*, September 26, 1999.

3   *Publishers Weekly*, August 23, 1999.

4   Robert McChesney, *Rich Media, Poor Democracy* (Urbana-Champaign: University of Illinois Press, 1999), p. 20.

5   Eugene Exman, *The House of Harper* (New York: Harper & Row, 1967).

6   James Hart, *The Popular Book: A History of America's Literary Trade* (New York: Oxford University Press, 1950), p. 88.

7   Janice Radway, *A Feeling for Books* (Chapel Hill: University of North Carolina Press, 1997).

8   Barbara Shrader and Jurgen Schebera, *The Golden Twenties* (New Haven: Yale University Press, 1988).

9   Book Industry Report of the Public Library Inquiry of the SSRC (New York: Columbia University Press, 1949).

10 Jean-Yves Mollier, *Louis Hachette* (Paris: Fayard, 1999), p. 305.

11 The Office of Strategic Services, the wartime predecessor to the CIA, kept close tabs on most of these exiles and their political preferences, maintaining extensive dossiers that can now be examined in the National Archives.

12 Pierre LePape, *André Gide, le messager* (Paris: Éditions du Seuil, 1997).

13 André Schiffrin, *l'Edition sans éditeurs* (Paris: Editions La Fabrique, 1999).

14 Pascal Fouché, *L'Histoire de l'édition française* (Paris: Bibliothèque de littérature française contemporaine, 1994).

15 Quoted by William Maguire in his *Bollingen, An Adventure in Collecting the Past* (Princeton: Princeton University Press, 1982), p. 61.

16 The popularity of the romance genre persists to this day: 201 million paperbacks were sold in 1998, the form of the reading matter having changed more than the content.

17 A marvelous and impressively fair account of these intellectual battles of the 1960s and 1970s can be found in Ira Berlin's introduction to Gutman's *Power and Culture: Essays on the American Working Class* (New York: Pantheon, 1987; New York: The New Press, 1991).

18 William Targ, *Indecent Pleasures: The Life and Colorful Times of William Targ* (New York: Macmillan, 1975).

19 J. William Fulbright, *The Price of Empire* (New York: Pantheon, 1989).

20 Ironically, the Simon & Schuster sales team initially guessed that these books, which became among the firm's largest commercial successes, would barely sell.

21 Michael Korda, *Another Life* (New York: Random House, 1999), p. 245.

22 Korda, p. 125.

23 From a talk given at the Small Press Center on March 24, 2000.

24 From an interview with the author in 1990.

25 See in particular a detailed and devastating *Fortune* article, "The Buzz Factory," by Joseph Nocera and Peter Elkind, July 20, 1998.

26 Book Industry Report of the Public Library Inquiry of the SSRC.

27 Bennett Cerf, *At Random* (New York: Random House, 1997).

28 Deng Maomao, *Deng Xiaoping: My Father* (New York: Basic Books, 1995).

29 Newt Gingrich, *To Renew America* (New York: HarperCollins, 1995).

30 André Schiffrin, "Publishers' Spring Catalogues Offer Compelling Reading about the Market for Ideas," *Chronicle of Higher Education*, March 19, 1999.

31 From the Wagenbach catalog, 1999.

32 McChesney, *Rich Media, Poor Democracy*, p. 202.

Index